::: PROMISING
::: AND GOOD
::: THE

PROMISING
AND
THE GOOD

Guy Mansini, OSB

Sapientia **Press**
of Ave Maria University

Sapientia Press
of Ave Maria University
24 Frank Lloyd Wright Drive
Ann Arbor, MI 48106
888-343-8607

Cover Design: Eloise Anagnost

Printed in the United States of America

Library of Congress Control Number: 2005903222

ISBN 1-932589-23-6

Table of Contents

Acknowledgments

I AM GRATEFUL to Lawrence J. Welch, of Kenrick-Glennon Seminary, Harry Hagan, OSB, of Saint Meinrad School of Theology, Mitchel Zimmerman, of the Diocese of Kansas City, Kansas, and especially to John C. McCarthy, of the Catholic University of America, for their criticism of earlier drafts of this book.

I wish also to thank the many classes of third year theology students at Saint Meinrad School of Theology on whom I have tried out various pieces of this book over the years in talking about the Church and priestly orders.

Introduction

THIS BOOK is about promises and why we should keep them. It is about what sort of thing we have to be in order to make promises and keep promises, and why it is natural for us to make promises. It touches on the kind of failure a broken promise is. All this is interesting in itself. But it is preliminary to the ultimate goal, which is to clarify what religious promising is, promising *before* God as in Christian marriage, and promising *to* God, as in the vows of the monk or friar. We should look at ordinary promising first, the promises one human being makes to another, before thinking about Christian promising. Also, between these two and as a necessary bridge, there is the promise God makes to us in Christ. It will turn out that we cannot imagine ourselves making the kind of promises we do in Christian marriage or in the vowed life except on the condition of that surety of his promise God gives us in Christ.

This book is not about the theology of the married state or of the religious state as such. It will not include a theology of the body. It does not repeat, but rather supposes some acquaintance with, the moral theology of the vows, such as used to be found in such things as Bernard Häring's *The Law of Christ*.[1] It does not make much call on the canon law of either marriage or the religious and clerical

---

[1] See vol. 2: *Special Moral Theology*, trans. Edwin Kaiser (Cork: Mercier Press, 1963), 281–96. The treatment of I. Aertnys and D. Damen is still widely available: *Theologia Moralis,* 17th ed. (Rome: Marietti, 1956), I, nos. 476–502.

states. It does not enter into recent discussions of the pastoral care of divorced and remarried Catholics.[2] Rather, this book is concerned more narrowly with promising, just as such. Of course, promising "just as such" cannot be talked about without attention to what it is that is promised, and it is the central concern of the book to point this out and to show why this obvious fact deserves very careful attention. Promising is the way one person realizes the good for another person and, in doing so, also for himself insofar as he is an agent of the good. Just so, we do not understand the promissory acts by which we enter the Christian life, or Christian marriage, or the religious or priestly life, without attention to the goods those acts embrace and the persons, divine and human, those goods are good for.

In what follows, our ultimate goal is to behold something of the splendor of Christian promises, including the promises of marriage and the religious life. The argument can be briefly expressed. The book moves from a philosophical to a theological appreciation of promising. After an introductory contrast of promising with predicting and promising with swearing (chapters 1 and 2), the issue of obligation is brought forward (chapters 3 through 8). Negatively, it is argued that the obligation to keep promises is not an artifact of the will of the one who promises. The point of departure of this negative argument is John Searle (chapter 3). Its course proceeds backward, from Searle to Hume and Hobbes (chapter 4), and then from Nietzsche (chapter 5) to St. Thomas (chapter 6). The argument then proceeds positively to explain that the source of the obligation of fidelity to promises is chiefly the good promised, and this obligation is identified with the love that St. Thomas describes as *complacentia boni*; moreover, the origin of the modern view, according to which the obligation is an artifact of the one who promises, is also considered by appeal to S. Pinckaers's treatment of Ockham in *The Sources of Christian Ethics* (chapter 7). In a role subsidiary to the

---

[2] See Kenneth R. Himes and James A. Corriden, "Pastoral Care of the Divorced and Remarried," *Theological Studies* 57 (1996): 97–123, for a discussion whose point of departure is the pastoral letter of the German Bishops of 1993.

good promised, we can recognize goods such as predictability and the strengthening of resolve that promising brings with it (chapter 8). The first part of the book concludes with a discussion of the effect of the modern view of freedom and promising on promises for life, such as marriage (chapter 9), and the manifestation of this modern view in the sociological theory of roles (chapter 10).

A remark on the relation between promising for life and Christianity introduces the second, theological, part of the book (chapter 11), and the deleterious effect on life promises of the privatization of Christianity is noted (chapter 12). The Bible is then interrogated on the topic of promising, and promising proves omnipresent in the Christian story of things (chapter 13). Our promises to or before God are seen to depend on his promises to us, which have some peculiar features, and divine promising is contrasted with human promising (chapter 14). The issue of what surety God can give us for his promises is addressed (chapter 15). Divine promising in the Old Testament is also contrasted with divine promising in the New. The Christological determination of promising is presented at some length (chapter 16), with special attention to St. Paul's Letter to the Galatians (chapter 17) and the Letter to the Hebrews (chapter 18). The point of all this is to bring forward the thesis of the first part of the book, now in theological attire. The goal is to see that the greater goods of the Christian economy invite us to an attention to promising and keeping our promising beyond that of the natural order. Furthermore, Christian promising is to be appreciated as a reception of our mission from Christ, and it is in this way our promising turns out to be good for him (chapter 19). This mission is first received in making baptismal promises (chapter 20). Next, Christian promises in marriage, the priesthood, and the religious life specify the mission taken up at baptism and share the splendor of Christ's keeping of his human words of promise both to his Father and to us (chapter 21). A contrast of Christian and pagan marriage turns on the goods each form of marriage envisages (chapter 22). The contrast between the dispensability of the vows of chastity and celibacy and the indissolubility of Christian marriage invites a comparison both of the structure of these promises and of the goods engaged (chapter 23). The nature of the priesthood as a calling to be embraced for life is noted (chapter 24). Last, the relation of Christian promise to the common good of the Church is noted (chapter 25). The epilogue takes brief stock of our situation as Christians in the modern West.

God's promising elicits hope. Hope is the opposite of despair. Despair is the sickness unto death. There is special reason, therefore, why this work should be "edifying," or, in the more recent translations of Kierkegaard, "upbuilding." "From the Christian point of view, everything, indeed everything, ought to serve for upbuilding" (Preface, *The Sickness unto Death*). ::

chapter one
Promising and Predicting

Promising and predicting both look to the future, but they are very different things. An initial contrast of promising and predicting will help us to see what promising is and to pick out some of its most important features.[1]

The difference is easiest to spot when we try to obscure it. This happens often enough when we set ourselves to break a promise. We say to ourselves and to our friends, "I made a mistake." The sense is, for instance, that I made a mistake when I married Sally; I thought things would work out well; but they didn't; I was mistaken. This is to assimilate promising to predicting. The point of doing so is to make a broken promise into a failed prediction. But the breakdowns are different, because the things breaking down are different. When I predict, I say what will happen, and my saying depends on my knowledge, perhaps some expertise, on my capacity to see beforehand what will happen later. But promising is not like that; it is not saying what will happen, but saying what I will do. The weather is predicted, and not promised, because the weather is not something that is done or performed.

Evidently, predicting can bear on all sorts of things, like the weather or next week's horse race or next month's election. So, it is not that predicting cannot bear on agents, on persons. If I predict the

---

[1] I owe the remarks in this chapter to a conference given by Mr. Gill Ring at St. Meinrad College on December 3, 1974.

outcome of the election, I am saying what many agents, many persons acting freely, will do. I may even predict how I will vote (although it is hard for an agent to predict what he, the agent, will do, without sounding pompous). On the other hand, promising to vote for my neighbor for alderman is evidently something different. When I predict, and misfire, I have made a mistake in calculation. We can say if we want that my word, my prediction, is no good. When I break a promise, my word is similarly no good. But also, I have "gone back on it," and we do not say that of a failed prediction. My prediction may not be backed up by events; but when I break a promise, it is I, and not the turn of events, refusing to back up my word.

Prediction is an engagement of mind, of intellect, but promising is an engagement of freedom and will. The failures of one and the other must be two different things. If I fail to predict the winner of the race or the turn of the weather, I fail as a handicapper or as a meteorologist. But if I fail to keep my promise, I fail as a human being. And this is why people getting set to break promises try to style it as a failed prediction. "I made a mistake." So, you may accuse me of bad judgment, but not of being bad. From our mistakes, we are to learn, and there is no shame is saying we have many things to learn. For being bad, for moral failure, we have to repent.

We can find the difference between promising and predicting in the very words. Predicting is "saying before" *(prae-dicere)*; promising is "sending before" *(pro-mittere)*. And what I send before, as it were, is myself as an agent. Predicting is a displaying of how things will be; promising is more like a doing—that is, it links me not to an event to be witnessed, but to an action, my action, to be done. When I predict, I imagine myself as registering some future happening, and I see myself seeing, looking at something. When I promise, I imagine myself as changing or arranging some future state of affairs; I see my hands. Predicting, as has been said, can bear on many things; promising can too, but it must always also bear on me as an agent, nor can I promise in someone else's place.

For all that they both look to the future, moreover, there is nonetheless a time difference to be noticed between predicting and promising, a time difference that concerns their outcomes, or fulfillments. Of course, I predict something before it happens; my predicting is in the past relative to what I predict. And I promise something before I do it; my promising is in the past relative to what I promise. But when my prediction is wrong, then we say "I made a mistake"—in the past tense; in the past, I miscalculated, misjudged, forgot to take something into account, and so on. When I break a promise, on the other hand, I break it now, and the breaking is a present thing for which I am responsible now, in the present. If, breaking a promise, I say, "I made a mistake," I am saying that the problem has already occurred and is done with. Prior to the moment of my speaking now, I miscalculated in the past, and there is nothing anybody can do about it, including emphatically me. But in fact, breaking the promise is something now; it is not something I did in the past. I can now, in the present, still keep it, if I want to. I was wrong then when I predicted wrongly. I am unfaithful, now, when I break the promise.[2]

Of course, it can be that one who predicts, predicts rashly, and so irresponsibly, and so his failed prediction also indicates a failure as a human being. This is so. The failure of mind is set up by a prior failure of will, a failure of freedom; it is a failure of responsible use of mind. Still, the very failure of the prediction is a failure of mind, not will, and one for which, in principle, I might not be responsible—no one, perhaps, could have predicted correctly in the circumstances.

We could say that, while promising and predicting are in the past relative to the content of the prediction or the promise, predicting remains past in a way that promising does not. Predicting stays in the past—I can continue to make the same prediction, but need not. Promising, on the other hand, is of its nature more mobile; it is supposed to go forward once the promise is made and accompany the one who promises. I have promised and, as we used

---

[2] Cf. J. L. Austin, "Other Minds," in *Philosophical Papers*, 3rd ed., ed. J. O. Urmson and G. J. Warnock (Oxford: Oxford University Press, 1979), 101, on knowing and promising: "Suppose that things turn out badly, then we say, on the one hand 'You're proved wrong, so you *didn't* know,' but on the other hand, 'You've failed to perform, although you *did* promise.'"

to say, "I am promised." The grammatical aspect of predicting is punctiliar, but the aspect of promising's tense is a present perfect. Promising, in the past, makes me different, and the difference is supposed to abide. I have predicted, perhaps, but am no longer predicting that same outcome—I have changed my mind. I rewrite the old report and issue an updated version of the forecast. But if I promised, and then am no longer promising that same thing, I am forsworn. It is as if I have perjured myself. ⸬

chapter two

::: Promising and Swearing

THERE IS ALSO a helpful contrast between promising and swearing. When I swear, I swear an oath. It may be an oath of office. I swear to discharge the duties of the office faithfully and honestly. That is, I promise to do so. Here, the oath attests to the truth of my word, a word that bears on the future, on my future action. But also, the oath I take may attest to the truth of my word just as such. I may swear that I will tell the truth, the whole truth, and nothing but the truth. My telling the truth can be considered a doing of something. But it is not a doing that directly and of itself changes anything. It is not like promising to make a payment, or to meet someone, or to live in a certain way. Telling the truth displays how things are, or how they were; it manifests, but does not change things. It is a light, not an action.

In a court of law, my oath that I will tell the truth bears ultimately on the past that I will be questioned about and that I am supposed to bring to light. Promising and predicting bear on the future. Predicting bears on a future that I expect will come to light—will be as I say. But I am not the one who makes the future so. Promising bears on the future, too, but as we have seen, it bears on a future I am to bring about.

Predicting and swearing are alike in that they are both concerned with displaying things. Predicting tries to light up the future. Swearing pursuant to testimony is ordered to lighting up the past. It

5

could be that I find myself predicting how someone will give testi-mony in a court of law. Even there, my immediate concern is with a future event, the action of the witness's giving of testimony, and it is only through that action that my concern reaches the past that will be lighted up by the testimony. By contrast, swearing my truthful-ness in court has as its immediate aim the display of actions or events that have already taken place.

When I swear to what someone has said, when for instance I swear that Tom said and declared such and such last month, my swearing evidently bears on the truth of what I am saying, not on what he said. I take hold of and present Tom's statement just in itself and more as a doing—he spoke these words—than as a dis-playing of what is the case. "He said such and such; but whether things really were so, you must decide." Even when it is my own past sayings that I am testifying about now, my swearing touches my testimony now, and not necessarily the truth of what I said then. I may swear now that I lied then.

The most important thing to see, however, is that swearing and promising are alike in a crucial respect, namely, that I am engaged as a person, and not just—as when I predict the weather—an expert. That is, as I engage myself to do something in promising, so I engage myself for the truth of what I say in swearing that some-thing is so. Swearing goes through a promise that I will tell the truth in order to end at the display of something. Promising goes through a display, a display of my truthful declaration, to an action.

It is true, there is such a thing as an expert witness. And such a witness may fail in two ways. Perhaps I give faulty meteorological or psychiatric opinion to the court, because I am not a very good weatherman or a very good doctor; I fail as an expert. But if, while being an expert, I lie under oath, and I tell what I know to be false weather information, or I falsify psychiatric reality, then I fail as a human being, not as an expert.

So again, like promising, lying under oath happens now, just as failing to keep a promise happens now. I may be giving witness as to what happened. But swearing falsely goes on in the moment of my telling falsely; it is not like the predicting of which we say, when it is not fulfilled, that it was wrong in the past. Swearing and telling the truth engage freedom and will, just like promising and keeping promises. Swearing and promising demand more of a person—they demand more person—than just predicting. They actualize more of the reality of a person. They put more of the person at risk.

This last point can be illustrated in two ways. In the first place, consider wagering—placing bets on the ball game, on the race, on the election. It was noted above that both predicting and swearing aim to display things. But why is it that the person is more engaged in swearing than in predicting? The contingency of the future and the inability of our faculties to divine it with certainty mean that no one undertakes either to guarantee or to receive a guarantee for a prediction.[1] But if I am witness to some action or word or event, then there is a kind of basic competence I am supposed to have just as a human being that comes into play. I ought to be able to remember what I saw, or said, or heard. I can engage myself, pledge myself, for the truth of what has been in a way that I cannot for the truth of what will be.

Wagering, however, moves predicting in the direction of swearing and promising. It makes it more interesting. It makes it more serious, so that the game can be played more intensely and enjoyed more thoroughly. Wagering puts me at risk in a way predicting does not. At least, it puts my money at risk, and if I bet foolishly, it may put lots more than that in jeopardy. Betting makes predicting more like promising. Of course, the wager consists in a promise to pay or do something if the prediction is wrong. But the promise is here parasitic on the predicting, which is basic.

In the second place, the personal engagement of swearing can be illustrated in the following progression of the ways displays are reported.[2] I can say, "It was George Sally married, not Scott." And I can say, "I know it was George Sally married, not Scott." And I can

---

[1] The prediction of an omniscient and all-powerful agent who transcends time and contingency would be something quite different, of course.

[2] Cf. J. L. Austin, "Other Minds," in *Philosophical Papers*, 3rd ed., ed. J. O. Urmson and G. J. Warnock (Oxford: Oxford University Press, 1979), 99–102, for a similar progression.

say, last, "I swear it was George Sally married, not Scott." Each
time, I display something in the world, the same something, that
Sally married George. The difference between the first and second
cases is that in the second I come forward with the known as the
knower who knows it, and accompany it into the light of speech. I
emerge as what Robert Sokolowski calls an "agent of truth."

> This use of the word "I" expresses the speaker as a person, a
> rational agent. Moreover, it expresses the rational agent as actu-
> ally exercising his rationality at the moment he uses the word.
> This use of the term "I" reveals the person of the speaker in its
> actual exercise, in its being-at-work as a person.[3]

The difference between the second and third cases, on the other
hand, is of quite a different sort. It seems to be a function of sin. If
no one lied, would anyone swear? According to the Sermon on the
Mount, anyway, the third form should be abandoned. "But I say to
you, Do not swear at all. . . . Let what you say be simply 'Yes' or
'No'; anything more than this comes from the evil one" (Mt 5:33,
37). That is, all our declarations of how things are should be true
and should be known to be true by those to whom we speak, such
that they do not need to be specially vouched for.

As to promising, I can say, "I'll go to the store for you." And I
can say, "I promise I'll go to the store for you." On the above anal-
ogy with swearing, there is no great difference between what these
forms accomplish; both display the agent undertaking the deed to
be done and his anticipation of doing it himself. On the other
hand, we probably do not want to say that promising would not
exist had Adam not fallen. There is a difference between these two
forms, to be sure, and we will see it in the next chapter. For now, we
must ask what the equivalent would be to the first form of displaying things. What is equivalent in promising for the bare form, "It
was George Sally married," in displaying? It would be something

---

[3] Robert Sokolowski, "Revelation of the Holy Trinity: A Study in Personal Pro-
nouns," in *Ethics and Theological Disclosures: The Thought of Robert Sokolowski*,
ed. Guy Mansini, OSB, and James G. Hart (Washington, DC: The Catholic
University of America Press, 2003), 167.

like, "You need someone to go to the store for you," or "Someone ought to go to the store for you." These statements pick out a benefit to be granted, a good to be achieved. They pick out an action to be done, but not the agent of the action. The one who says them has exercised his mind, but has not himself stepped up to the plate of action. He has articulated some practical truth, but not engaged himself for the good disclosed. It is that issue we will now begin to engage more fully.

THE CONTRAST OF PROMISING with predicting makes the role of freedom and will in promising salient, and this introduces the topic of obligation. I exercise not just my mind, as in predicting, but my choice, and it is as one who wants, wills, chooses, and is committed to act that I am obliged. Collapsing promising into predicting lets me escape the obligation to keep the promise I want out of, for there is no obligation to stand by a past prediction that turns out wrong the way there is to stand by a past promise that turns out difficult to keep. Again, the comparison of promising with swearing is not complete until we see that both touch on obligation, the one to do the promised thing, the other to tell the sworn truth.

But then, if promising obliges me in some way, how does it do it? What is the nature of the obligation? Where does it come from? Since promising is a function of will, it can seem that the obligation, too, comes from the will. There must be something right about that. How could I be bound to take the scouts to camp before I willingly said that I would? On the other hand, if we stopped there, if we said that my will generates the obligation, it would make it hard to explain how a promise could continue to bind after I have changed my mind about it, and want to change my will about it. If the promise and the obligation depend on my will, why cannot my will subsequently disengage me from the promise and the obligation? How can the will not be strong enough to destroy something that it produced? Why cannot I simply withdraw myself from my prior commitment? There must be something else involved.

There is a contemporary view to the effect that promising is a sort of magical act, and that the act of promising just of itself creates the obligation to keep the promise. I think John Searle adopts this view. The magic is in the idea that the will makes what it cannot unmake. Something seems to come from nothing, like the rabbit out of the hat, except that here, the magician cannot make the rabbit disappear into the hat again.

The indispensable analysis of promising Searle offers prominently involves thinking of promising as occurring by way of a "speech act." In this, he follows the trail blazed by J. L. Austin. To understand the idea of a speech act, speech as an act, we have to attend to what the uttering of words achieves beyond the mere uttering of words understood by both speaker and hearer. This last thing, the achievement of mutual understanding by the conveyance of sense and reference, Austin calls the "locutionary" force of words. There is also, however, an "illocutionary force" of words, an achievement of something beyond this conveyance, but in the very conveying it.[1] For instance, in saying "The cat is on the mat," the illocutionary force is that of assertion.[2] In saying, "I find the defendant guilty," the illocutionary force is that of rendering a verdict, and my action is a "verdictive."[3] In saying "I promise to go," the illocutionary force is that of promising, and the act is a "commissive." Additionally, "I promise to go" is a "performative" utterance. The idea here is that I am not only promising when I say "I promise" and so doing something, but I am also naming what I am doing as I am doing it. In the same way, "I order you to leave" effects

---

[1] J. L. Austin, *How to Do Things with Words,* 2nd ed., ed. J. O. Urmson and Marina Sbisà (Cambridge, MA: Harvard University Press, 1975), 94, 98–100. See Justus Hartnack, "Performative Utterances," *The Encyclopedia of Philosophy* (New York: Macmillan, 1967) for background.

[2] Austin, *How to Do Things,* 134, 139, with qualifications, 145–47.

[3] See the list, ibid., 151.

something, namely a command, and names what is going on as it is going on.[4]

It is not that Searle supposes the magic resides in the very words "I promise"; evidently, there may be no difference whatsoever between saying "Yes, dear, I will go to the post office for you tomorrow" and saying "Yes, dear, I promise to go to the post office for you tomorrow." Searle is well aware of that. I am not any more obliged by the second form than I am by the first form of words. We can make promises without saying the words "I promise," and Searle explicitly notes it.[5] In the same way, we can give a command to go simply by saying "Leave," without saying "I order you to leave."

From this we may conclude that what is achieved by way of illocutionary achievement may be achieved without its being named, and without my calling attention to it. Of course, sometimes it is nice to name what is happening as it is happening, and doing so can be an aid to clarity, and so also to the effectiveness of what is happening. It is by no means pointless to name such things as taking-for-my-wife in marriage, or thanking on Veterans' Day, or hereby appointing on the inception of office, and so on when they are happening. It adds to their publicity and can add to the intensity with which they are realized. The idea that the things cannot get done without the special forms of the language, however, is false, and these words are not required as are magical words.

Even so, Searle thinks the act of promising, with or without the words that name it in the very act of making the promise, just of itself creates the obligation to keep the promise. And I think his concentration on the force of words, illocutionary and even performative as they may be, contributes to this mistake. The very clarity and brilliance of Searle's analysis of the language, in other words, throws us off the track. It is especially noteworthy that he expressly excludes the idea that the thing promised is the source of the obligation, for

---

[4] John Searle, *Speech Acts: An Essay in the Philosophy of Language* (Cambridge: Cambridge University Press, 1969), 68. This is the same notion as Austin's "explicit performative," *How to Do Things*, 131, 150.

[5] Searle, *Speech Acts*, 55–56.

he maintains that conferring a benefit on the one to whom I promise is not the essential condition constituting a promise.[6] Even where what I am promising confers no benefit, or conveys no advantage or does no good, the promise, while "defective," is still a promise.[7] So, it cannot be the very thing that is promised that obliges.

The essential condition of promising, rather, is "that it is the undertaking of an obligation to perform a certain act."[8] Here, he says "undertake," but he says also that promises "create" obligations.[9] Also expressly excluded as the source of the obligation is the certainty with which the act may be counted on by others. "One may be tempted to think that promising can be analyzed in terms of creating expectations in one's hearers," Searle writes.[10] But that is a mistake. "Promising is, by definition, an act of placing oneself under an obligation."[11] By definition, according to its nature, promising generates obligation. To ask why we ought to keep promises is therefore "as empty as the question 'Are triangles three-sided?' "[12] That is just the nature of the "institution" of promising, as Searle calls it. "It is often a matter of fact that one has certain obligations . . . but it is a matter of institutional, not brute fact."[13]

Searle knows that we can ask whether or not we should accept the institution of promising, but he does not address the issue. If we did ask such a question, if someone asked why he ought to conform to the institution of promising, our resources would be slim. We could appeal to yet another institution. Or we should have to find some natural source of obligation. I mean here only that if the source of the obligation is not our institution, not our construction, not us, then the source can only be what is prior to us and our constructive activity, and that is nature. On the other hand, insofar as

---

[6] Ibid., 58–60.
[7] Ibid., 59.
[8] Ibid., 60.
[9] John Searle, "How to Derive 'Ought' from 'Is,'" in *Theories of Ethics*, ed. Philippa Foot (Oxford: Oxford University Press, 1967), 108.
[10] Ibid., 103.
[11] Ibid.
[12] Ibid., 108.
[13] Ibid., 112.

Searle's last appeal to found the obligation to keep promises is to an "institution," then he approaches what I have called the magical view of promising. Promises oblige because they oblige, and there is no more to be said. The obligation appears out of thin air, upon my "undertaking" or "creating" it.[14]

---

[14] For another exponent of the modern view, see Michael H. Robins, *Promising, Intending, and Moral Autonomy* (Cambridge: Cambridge University Press, 1984), e.g., 117: "on the position defended here, there are no natural rights or obligations prior to requirements that are created by the will."

chapter four

Hume and Hobbes
on Promising

S EARLE'S ACCOUNT is unsatisfactory because it is only a sort of remnant or shadow of a fuller account. This fuller account is hinted at, if not completely laid open to view, by David Hume.

His view is very close to Searle's. Hume does not speak of the will as creating an obligation, as does Searle, but this is a verbal difference. For both, promising and the obligation undertaken by promising depend on some institution and are conventional things.[1] Very pointedly, Hume says a promise is "*naturally* something altogether unintelligible."[2] For naturally, "morality depends upon our sentiments." In general, it is the sentiments of pleasure or pain that make for obligation; specifically, the obligation to perform some action seems to be nothing but the sentiment of displeasure at the idea of its nonperformance.[3] Promising, however, neither creates nor changes any sentiment of pleasure or pain; therefore, the obligation of it can be no natural part of morality.[4] The obligation must be an artificial one.[5]

---

[1] David Hume, *A Treatise of Human Nature,* ed. David Fate Norton and Mary J. Norton (Oxford: Oxford University Press, 2000), 3.2.5.6, 333: promises "have no force antecedent to human conventions," and see 3.2.5.10, 335.

[2] Ibid., 3.2.5.4, 332.

[3] Ibid.

[4] Ibid., and 3.2.5.1, 331: "The rule of morality, which enjoins the performance of promises, is not *natural*."

[5] Ibid., 3.2.5.6, 333.

The convention of promising serves mutual interest. It enables me to have confidence that, doing some service now for another, I shall not lose my future recompense, since he has promised. And did I not keep my own promises, no one would ever do me any service in the present without immediate transfer of payment. There is a sort of calculation of general and future benefits over particular and present costs of fulfillment of contract.[6] The idea is that, if I break the promise, no one shall ever trust me, and this will be injurious to my overall interest. Self-interest binds me to fulfillment of my promise, and a promise is "the sanction of the interested commerce of mankind."[7]

It is important to see that promising is for strangers. Friends do not make promises. When I make a promise, I am not acting from love or kindness as toward a friend. This is expressly excluded by Hume.[8] If love or kindness entered in, then promises would be things of nature, and the obligation natural. Promises are rather made in self-interest and satisfy the passions that regard the self, only, as Hume says, "in an oblique and artificial manner," that is, through the indirection of taking account of the interest of others.[9] Could we not rely on our promises to one another, we could never depend on the services of strangers. The convention is thus a very useful and necessary one, without which society would be unimaginable.

More particularly, Hume explains, the role of convention is to establish a sign, the words "I promise." If I give out the sign, then I do have a new motive, a motive to keep the promise, namely, self-interest, which has now been artificially put at risk by the convention.[10] So, it is illusory to think "willing an obligation" produces one.[11] That some new obligation might arise from the will is as incomprehensible and mysterious, in fact, as is transubstantiation or holy orders, "where a certain form of words, along with a certain

---

6 Ibid., 3.2.5.8, 333–34.
7 Ibid., 3.2.5.10, 335.
8 Ibid., 3.2.5.9–10, 334–35.
9 Ibid., 3.2.5.9, 334.
10 Ibid., 3.2.5.11, 335.
11 Ibid., 3.2.5.12, 336.

intention, changes entirely the nature of an external object, and even of a human creature."[12]

It might be said that Hume's attention to the sentiment attaching us to some good as it were prevents him from seeing the power of the good itself. He is express about what he does not see: obligation arises not from the willing of any "particular performance"— that is, the doing of some good thing—nor can it come from willing the obligation itself "which arises from the promise."[13] Also, there remains something obscure about the force of the obligation that convention establishes.[14] Is someone fitted out with the promiser's equivalent of Gyges's ring, by which he can break his promises with impunity, required to keep them?

If we turn to Hobbes, the obscurity in Searle's and Hume's appeal to convention vanishes. It is to be to be wondered whether both Hume and Searle suppose the truth of Hobbes's account, but decline to make us look, as Hobbes does, squarely at what he gives us to believe is the source of the obligation to keep promises.

Hobbes's view, the modern view of why we are obliged to keep promises, is expressed very clearly in chapter 14 of Book I of *Leviathan*. Here, we learn that it is the natural right of every man to do whatever it is in his power to do.[15] As whatever power that belongs to a man comes from nature, so also from nature is the scope of that power. However, Hobbes explains, this natural right of each man to do whatever his power extends to can be laid aside by renunciation or transfer. A man transfers a natural right "when he intendeth the benefit thereof to some certain person or persons."[16]

---

[12] Ibid., 3.2.5.14, 336.

[13] Ibid., 3.2.5.3, 332.

[14] At the end of the chapter, 3.2.5.15, 337, Hume argues that the conventional character of promises can be gathered from the fact that force invalidates contracts, force which "is not essentially different from any other motive of hope or feature, which may induce us to engage our word." This is as close as he gets in the chapter to the full modern account that we find in Hobbes.

[15] Thomas Hobbes, *Leviathan*, ed. J. C. A. Gaskin (Oxford: Oxford University Press, 1996), I, xiv, 6; 87.

[16] I, xiv, 8; 88.

A contract is a mutual transferring of right.[17] Where the contract calls for the deliverance of something or the performance of some act "in time to come," then "his performance is called keeping of promise, or faith, and the failing of performance, if it be voluntary, violation of faith."[18] When a man signifies a transfer of right by word or action, then "the same are bonds, by which men are bound to be obliged."[19]

This seems on the face of it to be what I have called the magical view of promising and have imputed to Searle. However, Hobbes explains, these bonds of obligation have their strength "not from their own nature (for nothing is more easily broken than a man's word), but from fear of some evil consequence upon the rupture."[20] The true and effective strength obliging the contracting or promising parties comes from "a common power set over them both, with right and force sufficient to compel performance."[21] That is, the true and effective strength is that of the sovereign. Promises bind, therefore, only in a "civil estate, where there is a power set up to constrain those that would otherwise violate their faith."[22]

It is true that apart from fear, Hobbes recognizes that glory and pride may also keep a man to his word. Unfortunately, this is not to be presumed on, "especially in the pursuers of wealth, command, or sensual pleasure, which are the greatest part of mankind."[23] Again, he says that if the fear of retribution at the hands of earthly powers holds us to our word, so also may fear of "spirits invisible."[24] But neither is the fear of God to be taken seriously in keeping men to their word. Invisible power, Hobbes says, is invoked by oath before God in making the promise. The oath, however, "adds nothing to the obligation." "For a covenant, if lawful, binds in the sight of God

---

[17] I, xiv, 9; 89.
[18] I, xiv, 11; 89.
[19] I, xiv, 7; 88.
[20] I, xiv, 7; 88.
[21] I, xiv, 18; 91.
[22] I, xiv, 19; 91.
[23] I, xiv, 31; 94.
[24] I, xiv, 31; 94.

without the oath, as much as with it." If unlawful, it "bindeth not at all."[25] Alas, there is no covenant, lawful or unlawful, apart from the establishment of the commonwealth, and so no covenant to swear to before God. Moreover, men have greater fear of retribution from earthly than from heavenly avengers, Hobbes says. The fear of God, if real, is then entirely superfluous.

It is the state alone that makes the obligation, therefore. Apart from the sovereign, apart from the civil state, men are still in the state of nature, and have made no real transfer of their natural right. In such condition, the scope of their natural power to do whatever they can remains undiminished. In such condition, I cannot reasonably expect one who has promised to do me some benefit at his expense actually to do it. For he has still the natural right to keep his good, or his time and energy, for himself, just according as he has the power to keep it. It will, moreover, be reasonable for him to keep it if I am not stronger than he. And contrariwise, if I were stronger than he, it would have been more reasonable for me in the first place simply to take from him what I wanted. As Hobbes summarizes in chapter 15:

> Where no covenant hath preceded, there hath no right been trans-
> ferred, and every man has right to everything; and consequently,
> no action can be unjust. But when a covenant is made, then to
> break it is *unjust*: and the definition of *injustice* is no other than *the
> not performance of covenant*. And whatsoever is not unjust is just.
>
> But because covenants of mutual trust, where there is a fear of
> not performance on either part (as hath been said in the former
> chapter), are invalid, though the original of justice be the making
> of covenants, yet injustice actually there can be none till the cause
> of such fear be taken away; which, while men are in the natural
> condition of war, cannot be done. Therefore before the names of
> *just* and *unjust* can have place, there must be some coercive power
> to compel men equally to the performance of their covenants, by
> the terror of some punishment greater than the benefit they
> expect by the breach of their covenant.[26]

---

[25] I, xiv, 33; 95.
[26] I, xv, 2–3; 95.

The nature of the obligation is therefore plain. It is my fear of the loss of an even greater good than the cost of fulfillment that moves me to keep my promise, or, otherwise expressed, it is my love of the good I now have and would lose that moves me to keep the promise. I sacrifice the smaller good of doing or paying what has been promised for the sake of the greater good—my greater good, that is—which the common power of the sovereign would take from me, if I did not do so. I calculate what most redounds to my own advantage, and act accordingly.

We might say, therefore, that what "obliges" is the good, what serves to my advantage, and that what moves me is love of this good. It seems better, however, to say that for Hobbes it is not the good that obliges, nor is there any obligation for me to love myself and what serves my good. That I love myself and my own and what serves me and them is just the way things are; by necessity of nature, I do love myself and what serves me. The fact of the matter is that I have these self-regarding desires; they are natural and ineradicable. I can more easily lop off a limb than change them. Obligation, on the other hand, is contrary to desire; it is not natural but something artificial and manufactured. It is manufactured by the erection of the civil state, of the sovereign power. It is not the good that obliges, but rather force, the power of the sovereign. The force in question, moreover—something that cannot be too often remembered in reading Hobbes—is physical, material force, the force that moves bodies and can wound living bodies, the force that can tie up, incarcerate, flog, the force that can hang, draw, and quarter. Moral constraint is really physical constraint. Moral obligation is the ligature of rope and chain.

Hobbes at least has the merit of clarity: the kind of obligation a promise has is the kind of obliging a man of superior strength can impose on a lesser mortal, or the kind of obliging the state can work through the power of police where, led off in handcuffs, we are "obliged" to stay in jail.

Hobbes makes the source of the obligation to keep promises as plain as a pistol. In fact, it is a pistol—and musket and pike. Searle and Hume before him speak less alarmingly, but also less plainly, of the "institution" of promising. But I think we may recognize in their "institution" the pale ghost of Hobbes's more robust Leviathan. Is the institution the artifact of mere words, or is it a configuration of force whereby power is deployed? If the former, then the institution of promising is as feeble as are the words of promising itself within the institution. Without arming the institution of promising with fire and sword, we must still wonder why we are obliged to keep our promises. ▪▪

::: *chapter five*
::: # Nietzsche on Promising

ANOTHER GREAT EXPRESSION of the modern view of the matter is offered by Nietzsche. Or, if we want to say that Hobbes gives us the modern, enlightened view, then Nietzsche gives us the postmodern view. Saying as much lets us anticipate what we will find in Nietzsche, namely, the unmasking of Enlightenment voluntarism.[1] In other words, it is Nietzsche's part to show us that behind what is presented as Reason there is only Will. In fact, this can hardly be said to be very masked in Hobbes, who for precisely that reason is not representative of his modern colleagues. For just think in how double-barreled a way Hobbes's view can be characterized. We might say that obligation is a function of reason for Hobbes: the obligation to keep a promise is the dictate of reason itself, where it calculates that more will be lost by breaking it. To break the promise is to be unreasonable. On the other hand, the object of reason's calculation here is naked, material force wielded at the behest of the sovereign. So, obligation is nothing but a matter of bowing, with more or less grace, to greater force of will. Reason's only part is to measure, first, how strongly I want something in comparison with something else, and second, how strong I am relative to another or to the sovereign.

---

[1] See Francis Slade, "Was Ist Aufklärung? Notes on Maritain, Rorty, and Bloom . . . ," in *The Common Things: Essays on Thomism and Education* (Mishawaka, IN: American Maritain Association, 1999), 48–68.

It is Nietzsche's part to destroy the illusion of reason so thinly overlaying Hobbes's account.

For Nietzsche, promising is straightforwardly a function not of commercial calculation, but of will, of power. It is a function of the will to power of the noble man, the man who surpasses in greatness (in power) all the little men of the mass who enter into political compact in order to produce Hobbes's Leviathan. Hobbes locates promising imaginatively in the political economy of the incipient bourgeois state. Nietzsche locates it in his construction, part historical recollection and part imaginative leap, of an antique noble society of warriors. Keeping the promise is a function, not of yielding to threat—that is the morality of the crowd, of the small men—but simply of carrying through one's will to do as one discovered one wanted to do in the past. That is noble. In other words, Nietzsche takes seriously what Hobbes does not, namely, glory and pride as motives to promise keeping. Even so, they are radically at one in their exaltation of Will.

In *The Genealogy of Morals*, Nietzsche speaks not of the obligation to keep promises, but rather of the "right to make promises." Much, if not all, is contained in this shift of perspective. Not everyone, he informs us, possesses this right, but only he who can carry out the promise. Only the one who has sufficient will, power, and capacity to master circumstances rightfully makes promises. Whoever has the right to make the promise will keep the promise; contrariwise, if the promise is broken, it was never rightly made in the first place. The "right to promise" is conceived as signifying the perfection of the individual's autonomy, freedom, and power. Society and the "morality of custom" are valuable only as means to the production of a man with such a right. They serve only to store up power in a man who by reason of his superior will and force therefore stands apart from, because above, the society and morality that produced him.[2]

Now, part of the capacity to keep a promise is the capacity to remember that the promise has been made; the right to promise

---

[2] Friedrich Nietzsche, *On the Genealogy of Morals,* trans. Walter Kaufman and R. J. Hollingdale (New York: Vintage, 1969), Second Essay, section 2.

depends on a sort of mastery of time. Or better, we should say it depends on a maintaining of self across time as the one who has pledged his word, his self. Mastery of time means mastery of self. Only they have the right to promise "who give their word as something that can be relied on because they know themselves to be strong enough to maintain it in the face of accidents, even 'in the face of fate.' "[3] Maintaining one's word in the required sense is more than a bare remembering. It means the subsequent determination of one's freedom in terms of the remembered word. It means making that word always alive. This is an achievement, and Nietzsche explains how it is accomplished as follows:

> wherever on earth solemnity, seriousness, mystery, and gloomy coloring still distinguish the life of man and a people, something of the terror that formerly attended all promises, pledges, and vows on earth is *still effective.* . . . Man could never do without blood, torture, and sacrifices when he felt the need to create a memory for himself; the most dreadful sacrifices and pledges (sacrifices of the first-born among them), the most repulsive mutilations (castration, for example), the cruelest rites of all the religious cults (and all religions are at the deepest level systems of cruelties)—all this has its origin in the instinct that realized that pain is the most powerful aid to mnemonics.
>
> In a certain sense, the whole of asceticism belongs here: a few ideas are to be rendered inextinguishable, ever-present, unforgettable, "fixed," with the aim of hypnotizing the entire nervous and intellectual system with these "fixed ideas"—and ascetic procedures and modes of life are means of freeing these ideas from the competition of all other ideas, so as to make them "unforgettable."[4]

And again:

> To inspire trust in his promise to repay, to impress repayment as a duty, an obligation upon his own conscience, the debtor made a contract with the creditor and pledged that if he should fail to repay he would substitute something else that he "possessed,"

---

[3] Ibid.
[4] Ibid., section 3.

something he had control over; for example, his body, his wife, his freedom, or even his life (or, given certain religious presuppositions, even his bliss after death, the salvation of his soul, ultimately his peace in the grave: thus it was in Egypt, where the debtor's corpse found no peace from the creditor even in the grave—and among the Egyptians such peace meant a great deal). Above all, however, the creditor could inflict every kind of indignity and torture upon the body of the debtor; for example, cut from it as much as seemed commensurate with the size of the debt.[5]

In the first excerpt, pain is self-inflicted. In the second, it is imagined as inflicted on oneself and those whom one loves. In one way, this is not much different than Hobbes. According to Hobbes, the obligation to keep a promise derives from the evil that will befall me if I do not. He collapses the obligation into the penalty clause of the contract, so to speak, which specifies the surrender of the pledge or surety that may be given upon making the promise. We should think of forfeiture of bond and escrow accounts. Nietzsche surmises, whether in jest or seriously, an altogether more immediately brutal function of giving pledge and surety. He goes behind the commercial machinery to the power over the body that is the real discipline of modern political economy. See the guilty executives led off in handcuffs. This power is exercised by the state for Hobbes. For Nietzsche, this sort of physical dominance of the body is self-administered. It is this that is the distinctive possibility of Nietzsche's view. Pain, self-inflicted at the time of the promise or to be imagined now and endured later if the promise is not kept, this is the mother of memory. How do I know the one who promises is trustworthy? Because he has hurt himself, or given himself to be hurt, if he fails. The one who promises as it were forestalls the state. He anticipates the sovereign's punitive measures, and so is sovereign of himself.

Later, once the kind of man who has a right to promise has been produced, the pledge of the word alone is sufficient, because the loss of himself, of himself as having the right to promise, will be more painful to the noble man than any bodily torture. His con-

---

[5] Ibid., section 5.

science will not let him break his promise. And conscience is strong, for it is nothing but the internalization of the law of compensation first articulated in terms of goods and bodily integrity, of pleasures and pains.[6] Where there are no men of conscience, and where there are no selves in Nietzsche's sense, however, then one will again require hostages before one accepts a word of promise.

If we sidestep Nietzsche's materialism (which by no means is to gainsay what he says of the connection between pain and memory), we are left with a remarkable appreciation of the kind of person it takes to make a promise, and of the engagement of the self in so making one. No matter that the content of the promise may be only some discrete act or the handing over of some extrinsic good, failure to keep the promise means far more importantly forfeiture of myself as having the right to make promises, forfeiture of myself as a certain kind of man, not just as honest and faithful—though that, too—but as being able to master time, to master myself across time, and remain the one who promised. And the pledge, no matter that it seem to be some possession or extrinsic good, is always therefore once again and more fundamentally myself.

Nietzsche's view gains credence from a common stratagem of one who wishes to escape his promise. When we want out, we say, "I'm a different person now" or "I'm not the same man I used to be." This seems to mean that somebody else made the promise, not me. The self who made the promise is lost, gone. The identity of the self has not been maintained across time.

In promising, therefore, for one who is serious, I promise at risk of myself. If in predicting I risk my powers of calculation and insight, my reputation as one experienced in the matter at hand, in promising I risk myself more completely. It is, just as Nietzsche says, a matter of my freedom, my agency or power, myself. The fidelity of the promise keeper is radically to himself. Nietzsche means the austerity of this view to impress and attract us.

Even so, and notwithstanding the things to be learned from Nietzsche, have we learned whence comes the obligation to keep

---

[6] Ibid., section 6.

promises? For Hobbes, it is the naked will of the sovereign, armed with the sword; for Nietzsche, it is the naked will of the one who promises, who has the right to promise, because he can afflict himself and is armed with the memory of his word. In either case, it is will.

::: *chapter six*
::: St. Thomas on Promising

To GET ANOTHER VIEW of promising and its obligation, we have to get back before the seventeenth century,
where we find Descartes and Suarez standing with Hobbes.
Descartes expressly considers promising as an abandonment of freedom, and anticipates the location of obligation in state coercion.[1]
Suarez, for his part, ties obligation to command and command to
the will of the superior.[2]

St. Thomas can serve us an accessible and authoritative witness
to a prior tradition. At first sight, it will not seem so, however. In
the great *Summa*, when he asks whether the promises we make to
God are binding, he says simply that the obligation to keep a promise is the obligation of fidelity: "ad fidelitatem hominis pertinet ut
solvat id quod promisit" (it pertains to the fidelity of a man to do
what he promised).[3] And answering the third objection, he remarks
that "obligatio voti ex propria voluntate et intentione causatur" (the
obligation of a vow is caused from one's own will and intention),

---

[1] René Descartes, *Discourse on Method*, trans. Laurence Lafleur (Indianapolis:
Bobbs-Merrill, 1956), 16.

[2] See the discussion of Suarez in Thomas S. Hibbs, *Virtue's Splendor: Wisdom, Prudence and the Human Good* (New York: Fordham University Press, 2001), 65–69.

[3] *Summa theologiae* II–II, Q. 88, a. 3, c. As a witness to the longevity of this view
in the Church's school, see C. Kirchberg, *De Voti Natura, Obligatione, Hones-
tate Commentatio Theologica* (Monasterii Guestf., 1897), 74: "Sicut formalis
ratio obligationis cuiuscumque voti est fidelitas erga Deum." And see his col-
lection of authorities from Scripture, the Fathers, and the theologians, 61–75.

and enlists Deuteronomy 23 in support, "propria voluntate et ore tuo locutus es" (by your own will and by your own mouth you have spoken). This would seem to be nothing but the modern view, the view we saw in Searle, to wit: the obligation of a promise is a product of the will of the one who promises.[4]

On the other hand, there are hints that things may not be so simple. In the first place, St. Thomas in part defines a promise as an ordination of reason: "est rationis actus, ad quam pertinet ordinare" (it is an act of reason, to which it belongs to order things).[5] If promising is an act of reason, how can the obligation be understood (exclusively, at any rate) as caused by the will?

Then there is the second part of the definition of a promise. The ordination of reason settles "quod ipse pro alio facere debeat" (what the one who promises should do for another). That may seem banal enough, but in so defining promising, St. Thomas expressly contrasts it with giving orders to or requesting something of another. "Just as a man by command or entreaty, directs . . . what is to be done for him by others, so by promising he directs what he is to do for another."

By a command, another becomes an instrument of my will, used unto my good. In promising, on the other hand, I make the good of the one to whom I promise my good. In promising, I am saying that I am making what is good for you—what will be good for you—a good for me to do. Your good is identified with my good. According to Robert Sokolowski, this is just the categorial form of friendship implicit in Aristotle's treatment of friendship.[6] What he means by this can be explained briefly, and it will be worth our while to understand Sokolowski's point. Categorial forms are

---

[4] Note that Richard N. Bronaugh, "Thomas Aquinas on Promises," in *The Medieval Tradition of Natural Law*, ed. Harold J. Johnson, Studies in Medieval Culture 12 (Kalamazoo, MI: Medieval Institute Publications, 1987), 5, recognizes the fact, if he does not approve of it, that St. Thomas's is not the modern view: "My conclusion will be that a natural law theorist, and Thomas in particular, cannot give to the act of promising any independent creative normative power." Right.

[5] *Summa theologiae* II–II, Q. 88, a. 1, c.

[6] Robert Sokolowski, "Phenomenology of Friendship," *Review of Metaphysics* 55 (2002): 459–60.

the structures in which we intend and articulate the world. They are the special concern of the phenomenological analysis of mind.[7] The categoriality of judgment, through which we intend that S is P, is perhaps the most familiar categorial object. But in addition to the contemplative categorialities such as that of judgment, categorialities in which the world is displayed, there are practical categorialities. Practical categorialities structure our mindful action. For instance, there are the proportional and arithmetic calculations that make for justice, distributive and retributive, and that Aristotle speaks of.[8] Also, there is the special work of mind—a categoriality—that enables us to deal with another person as a friend: this categoriality consists in counting my friend's good as my good. And it is the same categoriality operative in promising.

St. Thomas, for his part, makes benevolence, the intention of the other's good, central to the idea of friendship.[9] Friendship fully blown requires mutual benevolence, and mutually acknowledged benevolence. Still, the essential core is the intention to do good to the friend, to count what is good for him as a good that I will prosecute.

Taken formally, therefore, promising is an act of friendship, and we should not be surprised to find it characteristic of friends to promise things to one another. Perhaps many such promises fly beneath our radar, since we often do not name them as we make them. But, as it is characteristic of friends to live with one another, as Aristotle says,[10] so this living together generates daily occasion to undertake to do something for those we live with. This can be seen most easily within the friendships of marriage and the family. I mean to advert not so much to the foundational goods St. Augustine picks out for marriage—children, and fidelity, and the sacrament—but the smaller goods and services exchanged and re-exchanged, shared, planned for, promised, things like picking up the laundry and putting

---

7 For a discussion of categoriality, see Robert Sokolowski, *Introduction to Phenomenology* (Cambridge: Cambridge University Press, 2000), chapter 7.

8 Sokolowski, "Phenomenology of Friendship," 457.

9 *Summa theologiae* II–II, Q. 23, a. 1, c.

10 *Nicomachean Ethics* IX, 12.

gas in the car and balancing the checkbook and fixing the plumbing, things like helping with schoolwork and showing what is to be
appreciated in a novel and how to call turkeys, things like teaching
a child how to pray.

St. Thomas opens up an accounting of promising in the following ways, therefore. First, there is the question of promising as an
act of reason and as an act of will. Second, counting promising as an
act of friendship casts the "obligation" to keep promises in another
light. If we are inclined to imagine the obligation to keep promises
as something onerous, restraining, cramping, all of that disappears
when we think of the keeping of promises as an act of friendship.
Fidelity to our friends is an easy yoke. For friendship is founded on
love. And it is pleasant to do good things to those whom we love.
Love, moreover, is elicited by the good. And for the good man, it is
enjoyable to do good things for good people. The best things,
moreover, are goods that must be beheld by the mind, and to which
reason must order our actions. These are especially the intelligible
goods of the virtues, intellectual and moral, that perfect our humanity. We are happy to lead those we love to behold the world truly
and to act prudently and so lead them into their own happiness as
rational agents.

Insofar as we do think of the obligation to keep promises as
cramping, burdensome, rebarbative, we are moving within the
world defined by Hobbes. It is not that Hobbes's view is wrong so
much as it is partial. There are such things as commercial contracts.
But there are, or were, other things in the world as well. Hobbes's
view is not to be refuted, perhaps, so much as simply exposed, and
placed within a wider framework. Recall that Hobbes makes promising a calculation of utility. As Aristotle pointed out, utility or
advantage, meaning the calculation of what is good for me, can be a
basis for friendship. Like the mutual exchange of pleasure, mutual
advantage makes for friendship, too. But Aristotle thought the best
kind of friendship, friendship in its truest form, is based on virtue.
Now, friendships of utility have a structure different from that of
friendship of virtue. Friendships of utility share some of the same

structure of intentionality as do commands and orders. In commands, the ultimate concern is my own good.[11] In a friendship of utility, the ultimate concern is once again my good. As Aristotle remarks, "those who love each other for utility love the other not in himself, but in so far as they gain some good for themselves from him."[12] In friendship based on virtue, however, I love my friend for his own sake, and wish goods for him for his own sake. For his own sake, he is a rational animal, and the goods that befit him as such, for his own sake, are the virtues, the things that make him a more successful knower, a freer agent, a happier lover of the good. For Hobbes and for Hume after him, the paradigmatic promise is a sort of business contract, an act of friendship based on utility, where the ultimate intention of a contracting—promising party is his own good, his own advantage as measured, often enough, in goods and lands and money. For Hobbes, I am moved only by what redounds to my own good, and am ruled only by love of myself. In terms of a medieval distinction, there is only *amor concupiscentiae*, love of desire, and no *amor amicitiae*, love of friendship.[13] By "concupiscent love," I want things for my good. Friendly love here bespeaks friendship of the highest kind and wants good things for the other. St. Thomas lives in a larger world than Hobbes. A happier man, he lives in a world where one person may love another, and so be moved by the good to be done or given to a friend. Promising looks to be a different thing when this possibility of love is recognized.

---

11 *Summa theologiae* II–II, Q. 88, a. 1, c. I mean commands as to slaves or servants, living instruments of a master, whose good includes the good of his slaves as does a whole its parts; Aristotle, *Politics* I, 4, 1153b23–1154a17.

12 *Nicomachean Ethics* VIII, 3, 1156a11.

13 See *Summa theologiae* I–II, Q. 26, a. 4.

chapter seven

Promising and Obligation, the Good Promised

WHILE ST. THOMAS says that the source of the obligation to keep promises is the will, therefore, this may not mean what it would mean if Hobbes, or Searle, or Nietzsche said the same thing. What is will? For St. Thomas, it is intellectual appetite, appetite for the intelligible good.[1] It is the faculty of the Good, just as intellect is the faculty of the True and the Real. St. Thomas is certainly capable of saying, and does say, that our will binds us in making a promise. But there can be no such binding unless there is a good to be bound to, a good first grasped by mind, whose act it is to behold the order of our agency unto the goods that, once possessed, constitute the final and encompassing good of happiness. Will binds because it is an openness to the binding power of the intellectually beheld good. It binds because it is first bound. And this binding of the will is entirely . . . willing. It is according to will and not just by will. Will, intellectual appetite, is hospitable to this bond because hospitable to the good. And this bond, forged by the good itself and when it is perfect, is nothing more or less mysterious than love. What binds the will is love.

The contemporary language of obligation is most often used to indicate that someone owes something, is indebted in some way, and so is required to deliver or do something. The debts, the "obligations,"

---

[1] *Summa theologiae* I, Q. 80, a. 2.

are spoken of as something we "have." "Obligation" comes from the verb "oblige," which is more interesting, however. Here, someone is "obliged" because someone "obliges." Someone is to be credited, prized, thanked because his goodness actively obliges, in the sense that it forges the bond, makes the link. "He's an obliging boy" does not mean that he gives orders. It means that he pleases, is sweet tempered, prompt to help. The good he does calls to me, links me to him. And although it sounds a little antique, a little rural, we used also to be able to say, "Much obliged" in place of "Thank you." The good done, the help given, makes the obligation, the bond between the persons, not the will of the one who is in this way "obliged." The one who is obliged merely declares a fact, something established by the service rendered him by the one who obliges him, something established as well, perhaps, by the very goodness of the obliging man. And these two things, the good service done him and the goodness of the doer of this service, the one obliged can acknowledge or not according as he is or is not well brought up.

The obligation to keep a promise comes from where all obligation comes from, therefore, from the good. More particularly, the obligation to keep a promise comes from the good thing that was promised. Max Scheler sees this.

> In what concerns the obligating character of "promising" . . . the ought-to-be of what has been promised and of what has been accepted as such by the one who has been promised something has its foundation in the ought-to-be of this content.[2]

The obligation to go to the post office on someone's behalf comes from the good of doing just that thing. Promising does not make going to the post office an "ought to be," a "to be done," but connects me to it. More importantly, the obligation to have and hold Sally for my wife comes from just that very good of having and

---

[2] Max Scheler, *Formalism in Ethics and Non-Formal Ethics of Values,* trans. Manfred S. Frings and Roger L. Funk (Evanston, IL: Northwestern University Press, 1973), 531.

holding her for my wife—a good for her and, just as such, a good also for me. St. Thomas says, "that something ought to be done arises from the necessity of some end."[3]

The good of the thing promised controls. This is indicated by a common stratagem of one who is getting set to break his promise, and that is to minimize and trivialize what was promised. I promised I would take Tom to the fair. Subsequently, finding the prospect of so doing onerous or inconvenient, I start discounting the good of going: "The midway was bad last year; the exhibits will probably be boring," "Tom didn't really seem that interested," and so on. This diminishment of the good promised is what is going on when, about to get divorced, people say that marriage is "just a piece of paper," or, getting ready to leave the priesthood, one says "I haven't been such a great priest anyway; what difference will it make?"

Still, if it really is so evident that the good is the obliging, however did things become obscure to us? It is important to think how we got from the good as the source of the obligation to keep promises to the will as the source of this obligation. Servais Pinckaers would have us look at a change in the notion of freedom, a transition from what he calls "freedom for excellence" to "freedom of indifference."[4] The freedom of indifference is first privileged by William Ockham. It is a freedom where the will is absolutely unbiased, untrammeled, inclining neither to right nor to left. "What I mean by freedom is the power I have to produce various effects, indifferently and in a contingent manner, in such a way that I can either cause an effect or not cause it without any change being produced outside of this power."[5] This notion of freedom had, and continues to enjoy, an immense success. Lalande gives it as "the power to act with no other cause than the very existence of this power, that is to say, with no reason bearing on the content of the

---

3 *Summa theologiae* I–II, Q. 99, a. 1, c.

4 Servais Pinckaers, OP, *The Sources of Christian Ethics,* trans. Sister Mary Thomas Noble, OP (Washington, DC: Catholic University of America Press, 1995), 240–53, 327–53.

5 Ockham, *Quodlibet* I, q. 16, quoted in Pinckaers, *Sources,* 242.

act to be done," and again as "the indetermination of the will relative to its object."[6] Freedom for excellence, on the other hand, is
freedom as the faculty of the good. Freedom of indifference is freedom from the good. But freedom for excellence, far from indifferent to its object, is solicited by goods. Patient to reason, it is
determined—in the sense of modified—by the goods known by
reason; it is ordered by nature to the good and to happiness.

The interest in conceiving freedom as freedom of indifference is
to guard against determinism of any sort. Especially, fearful of intellectual determinism, we may want to emancipate the will from reason and reason's appreciative contemplation of the good. But, as
Pinckaers points out, this means a freedom that the Fathers and the
older masters of theology could not have recognized.[7] For them,
freedom was necessarily inclined to happiness, which consisted in
the maximal actualization of the human being's essential capacities
through the knowledge of the true and the love of the good.[8] It was
the freedom of a will naturally moved to the goods that perfect
man.[9] It was a freedom incapable of exercise prior to illumination
by intellect, the beholding of the good.[10] As well, it was a freedom
by nature ordered to use the passions and in using them make them
ordinate.[11] It was freedom that therefore flowered in temperance
and fortitude and was perfected in justice.[12] Inclined to a happiness
that, on the side of the subject, is constituted by the virtues, it was a
freedom whose proximate guide was prudence and whose ultimate
preceptor was wisdom. None of this was taken to imply that freedom in the sense of the ability to have done otherwise was not real.

---

[6] André Lalande, *Vocabulaire technique et critique de la philosophie* (Paris: Presses
Universitaires de France, 1976), 563.

[7] Pinckaers, *Sources,* chapter 15, "Freedom for Excellence," and chapter 16,
"Human Freedom according to St. Thomas Aquinas." And see the outline
contrast of the two freedoms on 375.

[8] For the inclination to happiness, see *Summa theologiae* I, Q. 82, a. 2, and at
length, the treatise on the last end, I–II, QQ. 1–5; for happiness as knowledge
and love, see I–II, Q. 3, a. 5, and Q. 4, a. 4.

[9] *Summa theologiae* I–II, Q. 10, a. 1.

[10] *Summa theologiae* I–II, Q. 9, a. 1.

[11] *Summa theologiae* I–II, Q. 59, a. 2.

[12] *Summa theologiae* I–II, Q. 61, a. 2.

But it was unthinkable that freedom could be threatened by the good, and it was understood that it was guaranteed by the finitude of the goods available for choice. No finite good could so absorb the will that the will necessarily inclines to it. The freedom of indifference, to the contrary, is threatened by the good and must be protected from it. Protection requires a freedom that is indifferent to happiness, to the passions, to the virtues, and, one may as well say, to human nature itself.

How can so alienated a will, so isolated a freedom, get connected to the good? And how will the moral law, whose authority is nothing except the authority of the good, any longer oblige? The last resort is the divine law, and that is where Ockham takes us. It is the divine law that connects the indifferent will to the good to be done. But this is obligation understood quite barely as the necessity to bend before another will, God's will. This is what replaces obligation as response to the beheld good. For the source of the moral bond cannot be God understood as good, holy, and deserving of all our love. That would be inconsistent, for then how could other goods not also solicit our love? No, Pinckaers says in explaining Ockham, "God's sovereign power over man created the moral bond. This bond had no other source than God's will, manifested with the force of obligation. A higher will thus exerted pressure and constraint on a lower one."[13]

Evidently, there is nothing for our purposes in Hobbes that is not already in Ockham. If it be the divine power that is the source of the obligation of the divine law for Ockham, Hobbes says the same: "The right of nature, whereby God reigneth over men, and punisheth those that break his laws, is to be derived, not from His creating them, as if He required obedience as of gratitude for His benefits; but from His irresistible power."[14] Not from God's creating them—then should men be responding to the generosity of the Good in discovering the created good that they themselves are and that he gives them. But no. In Ockham as in Hobbes after him, the obligation to

---

[13] Pinckaers, *Sources,* 343.
[14] *Leviathan,* II, xxxi, 5; 237.

keep promises can come only from power and will. It might be God's will, or the will of the sovereign, or my will. It might be God's power, or the sovereign's power. In these cases, promising constrains, and is a limitation on the future exercise of my freedom of indifference. This is why it is Nietzsche alone who makes of promising something attractive to modern man: promising is a matter of my power and its manifestation and not a matter of submitting to an alien power. It remains that it is still a matter of power.

But within the older view, promising is not constraint and diminishment of freedom, but the flowering of it, an expression of the love that is freedom's central act, an achievement, a realization of the self in the only way a finite, created self can realize itself, by giving itself to the good that it does not create, but can only find, discover, and receive with thanksgiving.

For St. Thomas, the good changes us; it makes us better. When we see it, the good conforms us to it, proportions us to it. He speaks in this context of a *coaptatio* or *habitudo* unto the good, a relation to the good worked in us by the good itself. He calls it *complacentia boni*, but if we say "complacency of the good" in English, we have to think the Latin, and understand a pleasure in and a resting in the good that is worked in us even before the good is possessed. It is an ordination to the good, a link, a bond. It is the fixing of the appetite in the good.[15] It is the spring of action ordered to the acquisition of the good. But just in itself, before deliberation, before choice and action, it is the suasion of the good, the obliging of the good, obligation. Yet another name for it love. And that is what St. Thomas calls it, "love," the first information of appetite by its object.[16] It is "first" in that it is prior to desire, which stretches toward an absent beloved, and "first" again in that it is the foundation of enjoyment,

---

[15] *In III Sent.*, d. 27, q. 1, a. 1, resp.: "quando affectus vel appetitus omnino imbuitur forma boni quod est sibi objectum, complacet sibi in illo et adhaeret ei quasi fixum in ipso; et tunc dicitur amare ipsum."

[16] *Summa theologiae* I–II, Q. 26, aa. 1 and 2; see St. Thomas's commentary on *The Divine Names* of the Pseudo-Denys, chapter 4, lectio 9. For modern discussion, see Frederick E. Crowe, "Complacency and Concern in the Thought of St. Thomas," *Theological Studies* 20 (1959), 1–39, 198–230, 343–95.

which flowers when the beloved is present. And it is "information." That is, it bespeaks the change, the shaping and forming, that the good works on our nature, the perfecting of our rational nature that takes place precisely in such shaping.

For Hobbes, recall, obligation is an artificial work, for there is no obligation prior to the social compact. Insofar as it is based on nature, it is based on fear. For St. Thomas, obligation is the most natural thing in the world, for nothing is more natural than love. It is hard to imagine two more different visions of the universe. ⁝⁝

chapter eight

Promising and Obligation, Other Goods

I T CAN STILL SEEM that something must have been over-looked in the previous account of promising and obligation. Is there not something special to promising itself, in addition to the thing promised? Was I obliged to go to the post office before I promised I would? Does the act of promising not add something to the good of the thing promised? The last two questions are distinct, and we can begin with the last one.

Yes, promising adds something; it adds three things to the thing promised. In the first place, it adds the good that other persons can now count on the post office stop being made. It makes the good of going to the post office for Sally something that can be counted on—by Sally, and by, say, Sally's daughter who would have to go if I did not. It is important to see, however, that this good is there independently of my will, just as is the good of going to the post office itself. Its realization depends on me, but that does not mean my will makes the good to be the good it is, and it does not mean that my will makes the obligation of the promise.

Moreover, it is the sovereignty of the good, the fact that it is the good that generates the obligation, that explains why, if I have George go to the post office in my place, no one will think I have failed to keep the promise. Yes, I said I would go. But it is the good and its realization that controls, and so George can go in my place with no shame on me.

Of course, there are some promises in which I am not replace-able, for there are some goods, and so there are some things prom-ised, in which I am not substitutable. The important promises are like that. These are the promises where, in a way, the thing prom-ised is myself, or a way of being myself. So, I cannot commission another man to fulfill my marriage vows. This is so, it should be noticed, not just because of circumstances. It is not just because no one else is available, as may be the case for checking the post office, in which case I have to go. No, it is rather a matter of the nature of the thing. In marriage, for instance, the partners promise themselves to have and to hold, and no one else can do their promised having and holding for them.

Despite the unsubstitutability of the one who promises mar-riage for the carrying out of the promise, marriage promises show in another way even more clearly that the obligation derives princi-pally from the good promised. Such promises are suitably styled "life promises." In such promises—again, think of marriage—one of the extra goods picked out above, the good of being able to count on the promised good, is built into the promised good. The nature and qualities of such promising will be taken up later. Here, it is enough to say that in such promises as marriage the whole life is promised, not some discrete act in the future, and that the good of marriage is in part constituted by the note of surety announced by the "till death do us part." The good and the note of surety are not separable as are in principle going to the post office for someone and the good of the person being able to count on that service being performed the day before it is performed. In the same light, it is to be noted that the discharge of the marriage promise—keeping the promise—begins immediately; it is not something separated from the promise itself by a temporal gap.

This good, the certainty of the good to come, is what St. Thomas is getting at when he says that the obligation to keep a promise is the obligation of fidelity. By my promise, I instill an expectation in the one who receives the promise. According as I really do have the capacity to keep the promise, and according as I really am a truthful person, the expectation is legitimate. This introduces a distinct note of justice into promising, a feature that becomes prominent especially in contracts.

The good just pointed out belongs to the one to whom the promise is made. There is also a second good that accrues to the fundamental good of the thing promised by promising, and it belongs rather to the one promising. This good is the kind of stability of the will that promising effects. Promising fixes my will on the good promised. "Vovendo voluntatem nostram immobiliter firmamus ad id quod expedit facere" (by vowing we fix our will immovably on what it behooves us to do).[1] It is for this reason, St. Thomas says, that Christ did not make any vow; his will to do his Father's will could not be further strengthened by a promise.[2] Our will, by contrast, is often capable of, and often needs, further strengthening in resolve.

This second good is readily understandable for temporally stretched out agents such as we are. For such stretching brings with it the possibility of forgetfulness. And while it is certainly necessary to forget some things, as Nietzsche pointed out, it is good to remember others. Time covers over what once we saw. More properly, our imperfect act of attention does not keep the good vividly present to us. The good may not always shine before us and show itself to us in its first beauty. In such an eventuality, remembering our promise, we remember, if not the good itself, at least the fact that once the good in question convinced us—conquered us—and we are provoked to wonder, to look again at what once we must have beheld more clearly, more fully. We are moved to look once again at what once held us in its attracting power more perfectly. If making promises is a matter of letting the good have its way with me, then keeping them is matter of letting it keep its sway over me. The keeping is just the making extended. It is a matter of continuing to be mindful of the good so that it may move me as at the time of the promise. Nietzsche is right to say that "the right to make

---

[1] *Summa theologiae* II–II, Q. 88, a. 4, c.
[2] *Summa theologiae* II–II, Q. 88, a. 4, ad 3.

promises" requires memory. And yes, it requires memory of self. But especially, it requires memory of the self as hospitable to the good—memory of the good.

Then, third, there is one more good that accrues to the fundamental good of the thing promised by promising. This good is a function of the public character of promising, which of its nature, to be sure, can be pretty variable. The idea here is that when I promise to do something or undertake some work, by that very act of promising, I display the thing undertaken as a good, and this display is itself something good. Promising, because of its public character, is a display of all the things so far mentioned as good: the basic good of the thing promised, the good of certain expectation, the good of stability of will. Making a promise reveals me as acknowledging the good in question, and the good of predictability, and the good of fixity of will, and makes others mindful of these things as well.

In the display of the three goods just mentioned, there is also displayed the good of the persons as such, which we might think of as the terminal goods of promising. First, there is manifested the good of the one promised, the good that he is as a person, and perhaps also the good of his character. He is one who, as a human being or as a good human being, is worthy of having some good given him or done for him. Second, the good of the one who promises also stands forth. In promising, he shows himself as appreciating all the goods in question, especially, as responding to the good of the other, and as competent to effect what is good for him. He stands forth as both an agent of truth and an agent of good, one on whom the good depends. It is given in promising for the giver and receiver of the promise to behold one another in just these ways, under these formalities, and we enter here part of the territory of love and friendship.[3]

There is still the other question with which this chapter began. If the obligation derives from the good of the thing promised, am I obliged even before I promised? The answer is that in some cases I

---

[3] I owe the content of this paragraph to John McCarthy.

certainly am; some promises bear on what I am morally obliged to do whether I promise or not. So, my promise to tell the truth does not create the obligation to be truthful, and failing to make the promise or keeping my fingers crossed does not relieve me of the obligation either in a court of law or in the public square. It may be also that I am obliged to perform quite ordinary acts for those I live with or am friends with. If my elderly relative has no real means of getting to the doctor except me, I am obliged to take her or to provide such means.

Why then promise in such a situation? There remains the good of the certain expectation aroused in those concerned about and connected to the event, and there is the good of shoring up the stability of my will. Promising in such circumstance is therefore by no means otiose. It is a realization of friendship.

On the other hand, the thing promised may be something not already antecedently required of me. Then my promise makes it required, and once again, the thing to look at is certainty of others' expectation, which of itself is a good weighty enough to oblige fulfillment of the promise. Here, it is important to recall the distinction already noted between promises in which I am and promises in which I am not substitutable as the one who carries them out. In those cases where my promise alone makes me the responsible agent, but where in principle someone else could accomplish the good in question—in those cases, we can think of promising as nothing more than designating the hitter of a ball that anyone can hit but that has to be hit by someone. It must be that someone take my elderly relative to the doctor. Whoever says he will steps up to the plate, and there must swing.

And what of cases where the thing promised is evil? Then there is no obligation at all. A promise cannot make me obliged to perform a morally evil act. Herod's promise to give Salome anything, "whatever she might ask" (Mt 14:7), did not extend to the head of John the Baptist, for this was not something that could justly be asked for. If we are to think of Herod as having any moral sense whatsoever, on the ground that, after all, he was loath to do as the girl asked, then it was befuddled by the vanity and extravagance of his words of promise before a corrupt court, and under the cloak of a promise he did a foul deed. He mistook corrupt public opinion for display of the good. He mixed up a firm will and a just will.

The various goods at stake in promising, and how they bind, can be illustrated nicely from William Faulkner's *Go Down, Moses*, the story of Isaac McCaslin's inheritance from his Uncle Hubert Beauchamp:

> there had been a legacy, from his Uncle Hubert Beauchamp, his godfather, that bluff burly roaring childlike man from whom Uncle Buddy had won Tomey's Terrel's wife Tennie in the poker-game in 1859—"posible strait against three Treys in sigt Not called"—; no pale sentence or paragraph scrawled in crippling fear of death by a weak and trembling hand as a last desperate sop flung backward at retribution, but a Legacy, a Thing, possessing weight to the hand and bulk to the eye and even audible: a silver cup filled with gold pieces and wrapped in burlap and sealed with his godfather's ring in the hot wax, which (intact still) even before his Uncle Hubert's death and long before his own majority, when it would be his, had become not only a legend but one of the family lares . . . two weeks after his birth in 1867, the first time he and his mother came down stairs, one night and the silver cup sitting on the cleared dining-room table beneath the bright lamp and while his mother and his father and McCaslin and Tennie (his nurse: carrying him)—all of them again but Uncle Buddy— watched, his Uncle Hubert rang one by one into the cup the bright and glinting mintage and wrapped in into the burlap envelope and heated the wax and sealed it and carried it back home with him where he lived alone now without even his sister either to hold him down as McCaslin said or to try to raise him up as Uncle Buddy said.[4]

The good promised is the substantial means with which a young man enters into his majority, and the freedom of action such a

---

[4] William Faulkner, *Go Down, Moses, in William Faulkner, Novels 1942–1952* (New York: Library of America, 1994), 226–27.

legacy bestows on him. Upon Beauchamp's promise, moreover, this good is expected, and counted on, and that makes another good. This good is enjoyed as Isaac and his mother and cousin McCaslin Edmonds visit Uncle Hubert over the years, and inspect the burlap bag, and feel its heft, and assure themselves it is still there, waiting for Isaac to take possession of it.

Was Beauchamp obliged to arrange the legacy? He is not obliged to promise a silver cup and fifty gold pieces. He is not obliged to arrange a legacy as such. But he has obligations to Isaac. He is Isaac's uncle, and Isaac's father is dead. Beauchamp undertakes, as it were, to give a determinate shape to his obligations by arranging the legacy.

There is, third, the good of Beauchamp's resolve to see the legacy through, which is displayed to us by its decay. The stability given to Beauchamp's will by his promise is shown to us in its decline, as early withdrawals from the cup are noted on linen bond and at a promised five percent, and subsequent ones on any scrap of paper to hand, until the silver cup itself is replaced by a tin coffee pot.

Fourth, and the good Faulkner's description most of all brings to light, there is the good of the display of these previous goods, as Beauchamp rings the coins into the cup and seals cup and coin in front of the family. The cleared table, the bright lamp, the gathering of the family in witness, the telling of the coins one by one, the glint of silver and gold, the savoring of the event afterward, and its subsequent legendary quality—all conspire to evoke the splendor of the good itself, to make its beauty shine.

chapter nine

Life Promises and the Freedom of Indifference

IT IS HARDLY to be thought that human beings could live together and not make promises. The bonds of affection, and the need to plan ahead, make it unthinkable that there should not be the multitude of ordinary promises, more or less explicit, about more or less weighty matters, that make up the warp, already laid out, reaching into the future, onto which are woven the actions of daily life in the family, the neighborhood, the workplace and marketplace. As to what have been called "life promises," the promises that make marriage or religious life, that is another question. In this chapter, we will first consider some of the peculiarities of life promises, and then see how the modern appreciation of freedom makes such promises hard. Third, there is a curious part of the experience of choice and promising that seems to support the modern sensibility. Last, Iris Murdoch offers an insightful description of this sensibility.

In the previous chapter, certain differences of these promises from ordinary undertakings were noted by the way. First, yes, they engage for life, not for some discrete action or work in the future. Second, their fulfillment begins as soon as they are made. Third, the agent who makes them is not substitutable—George can go to the store for me, but not be the husband of my wife for me. If he is the husband of my wife after my decease, he fulfills his promise and not mine.

As to the first note, life promises engage and presuppose a capacity, not just to look ahead, but to look ahead to the end, and so conceive of life as a whole. We cannot shape our origins, but we can, within limits, give shape to our end. The transcendence of time—from within time—that such promises bespeak reveals the whole complexity of man, metaphysical and moral. Metaphysically, this transcendence of time is spirit, but as exercised only from within time, it is also bodily. Morally, a choice, a decision that in such promising intends the whole can itself be but a sketch, an outline. It is not immediate possession of the intended, but a mere stretching toward it. It is more empty than full, and the filling requires many trips to the well. The transcendence of time so exercised and called on, the metaphysical complexity it reveals, the moral possibility it enables, is absolutely central to how we think of ourselves, to what we think ourselves to be. At least, it has been.

Because of the seriousness of a promise for life, and notwithstanding the fact that fulfillment does not wholly and properly begin until the promise is made, there can be a kind of practice session for life promises. Sometimes, even before the promise is made, one undertakes some part of the duties of the promised state. For married life there is the period of engagement. For religious life, there is the time of simple vows. In both, the promised good is realized not just imaginatively but, in some measure, really. True, fulfillment is of a different tone after the promise itself and begins truly only with the promise. Still, as life promises anticipate the whole of life, engagement and simple vows anticipate this anticipation.

The second note, that fulfillment begins as soon as a life promise is made, means that we can fail in two ways. There is the manifest and calamitous and all at once evident failure of desertion, divorce, disappearance. There is also the more hidden, slower corrosion of silent nonfeasance. We do not leave, but then, we do not love either. We stay together in body but not in mind. The promise remains a thing of imagination, but is not realized in the only way it can be realized, which is to begin now to fulfill it. The realization of the project of transcendence is not sought in the only place it can be sought, in the here-to-hand circumstances of life.[1]

The third note, the unsubstitutability of the one who makes the promise, suggests a sort of ranking of promises, as has been noted. The more I cannot find a substitute, the more weighty the promise. Marriage vows are not like promising to give a lecture, and promising to give a lecture is not like promising to take someone to the doctor. The note of unsubstitutability in life promises also leads to the mysterious question of destiny. Was I born to make this life promise? Without supposing I would not have married had I not met Sally, and without supposing there might not be five or five thousand others I might have married and married suitably, still, was our marriage made in heaven? That is, was it meant to be by a Mind, designed by Providence? If I could have married another, made some other life promise, still, the one I have made makes me. The impossibility of imagining concretely and convincingly how I might have been quite . . . *other* than I am seems to make life promises a curious mixture of freedom and fatality.

Or so it used to be. Some people think that the promises that make for marriage or religious life or the Catholic priesthood are more rare than in former days, that they are especially hard to make today, that the kind of life they constitute is especially in danger. It is difficult to have a good opinion about whether this is so. One reason for thinking it so, however, is that some people think such promises are wrong. Clever animals do not need, and perhaps should not attempt, to contract anything for life. We are distinguished from the birds by figuring out how to fly higher than they, and from the mole by devising tools to dig deeper. But counting out the eons and dividing the nanoseconds does not get us off the earth. Perhaps it is puffery to vaunt ourselves on our "time transcending" capacity when all we need look for and all we should count on is a Roth IRA. Could we imagine the friends and roommates who

---

[1] Kierkegaard knows this state of affairs as the "despair of infinity"; see Søren Kierkegaard, *The Sickness unto Death,* trans. Howard V. Hong and Edna H. Hong (Princeton, NJ: Princeton University Press, 1980), 31–32.

inhabit the network sitcoms making life promises? And if these characters amuse us, can our own possibilities be more than trivial?

If it is a fact that life promises are somehow more difficult to make today, it would not be hard to put our finger on some likely explanation. Beyond the sort of crass materialism just alluded to, two things in particular can be pointed to. There is the effect of thinking of freedom as freedom of indifference, and there is the waning of Christianity.

Freedom understood as the liberty of indifference makes trouble for promising of any sort, but it makes an especially heavy weather for life promises. If the liberty of indifference be conceived as the chief and overriding good, it withers our ability to promise at the root. Is it so conceived? Not by Ockham, whose world is filled with many good things. It is conceived in that way by moderns, however. Pierre Manent explains how this came about. In wishing to free themselves from Christianity and the supernatural, modern political philosophers conceived that they had also to free themselves from nature itself.[2] If nature—human nature—remains, then of course the finality of that nature remains. And the finality of a nature is toward natural ends, ends that are naturally desired. Why should this be a problem for those wanting to free themselves from what is added to nature by grace and wanting a political isolation of the Church more successful than that proposed by Dante and Marsilius of Padua? The rejection of grace requires an attack on nature because natural desire for natural good is as it were the place where we recognize supernatural goods as the surpassing goods they are when they are proposed to us. Supernatural goods, moreover, provide a super-satisfaction of natural desire. If the Church that dispenses grace and promises a supernatural happiness to man is not to return to political hegemony, then nature itself must be destroyed.[3] This means that there can be no natural ends soliciting our will, no goods man is oriented to by a natural law that is more than descriptive. The only

---

[2] Pierre Manent, *The City of Man,* trans. Marc A. LePain (Princeton, NJ: Princeton University Press, 1998), 25–26, 170–71.

[3] Ibid., 198.

"good" that remains is freedom itself, now newly and by nature indifferent to all goods, free to become creator of all values.[4]

It is true that, in the course of this history, freedom of will itself, understood as a freedom in virtue of which the agent could have done otherwise even were nothing changed in him or in his situation, is abandoned for modern materialism and determinism. This is nothing to the purpose. The point is to free the will from ends, ends and therefore goods naturally or supernaturally knowable, and so also from any human authority that would pretend to direct another human being on the ground that it knows these goods.[5]

If such freedom, indifferent to natural ends so as to be more patient to felt desire, really is the great and best thing, the thing that makes us ourselves, why diminish it by promising? How diminish it by promising something for life? Such a promise would be the alienation of freedom itself. Why sell one's self into slavery? What would it profit a man to gain a wife and children, hearth and home, at the price of his very soul, his freedom always to start over and light out, again, for the territory? On this view, life-promising seems foolish, and, if we have a duty to keep our selves whole and undiminished, immoral.[6]

It can be observed, moreover, that there is a part of the experience of deciding, especially promising something for life, that is heightened by thinking of freedom as freedom of indifference and that in turn makes such a definition of freedom plausible. In any choice among a field of possible chosens, our initial experience is of a fullness of possibilities out there in front of us. Since all are possible for us, we feel especially potent, powerful. Choosing means narrowing the field, cutting away, cutting down, to just one. And this seems to be a narrowing and diminishment of ourselves, of the agent choosing. Or again, by our being tied to one, our freedom of

---

4 Ibid., 171ff. For a very brief expression of this argument, see Manent's "Christianity and Democracy," in *Modern Liberty and Its Discontents*, ed. and trans. Daniel J. Mahoney and Paul Seaton (New York: Roman and Littlefield Publishers, 1998), 101–3.

5 Manent, *The City of Man,* 156–57.

6 John Paul II considers the freedom of indifference in *Veritatis Splendor*, 32, 34.

indifference is diminished, and if that is what we are—freedom so described—then we are diminished.

Of course, the truth of the matter is that we only become something real and actual by choosing one course, only one, from the field of many possible but hardly compossible courses. The experience of diminishment is real enough; it comes from the contrast of a fullness of possibilities with the narrowness of one actual course. But the many possibilities are not possible of all being realized together. One course alone can be achieved, realized, and made actual—only if chosen. Fullness in fact lies with the choice of one, not with the fantasy life of living in possibilities. Not to choose because of a fear of diminishment is what Kierkegaard knows as the "despair of possibility." It is the despair especially of aestheticism, of that kind of life that in its lowest form is regulated by the irregularity of whatever desire is present, by the strongest passion now at hand. And it seems especially to describe the effects of a moral sensibility determined by thinking of freedom as freedom of indifference.

> This self becomes an abstract possibility; it flounders in possibility until exhausted but neither moves from the place where it is nor arrives anywhere. . . . Thus possibility seems greater and greater to the self; more and more becomes possible because nothing becomes actual. Eventually everything becomes possible, but this is exactly the point at which the abyss swallows up the self. It takes time for each little possibility to become actuality. Eventually, however, the time that should be used for actuality grows shorter and shorter; everything becomes more and more momentary.[7]

The experience of diminishment upon choice, any choice of some one thing from out of a field of possible chosens, is therefore the ground of a dangerous illusion. To keep all our possibilities open is never to amount to anything.

This illusion is all the more powerful where the freedom of indifference is prized as the essence of the self, and where nature and natural ends are denied. The idea that anything could be worthwhile

---

7 Kierkegaard, *Sickness*, 36.

for a life is blocked, for there is nothing good antecedent to our deliberation and choice for which we should lay aside our indifference and relative to which we should become different forever. And the very experience of "diminishment" can seem to confirm this judgment. This is not to say, however, that there cannot be goods, better called "values," consequent to and dependent on deliberation and choice. Just as the idea that promising is beholden to the good, and that the obligation to keep a promise is generated by the good promised, is part of the larger idea of the sovereignty of the good generally over all our endeavors, so the idea that promising by itself generates the obligation is part of a larger view according to which the will generates all value whatsoever. This view can be considered the complete working out of the idea that freedom is freedom of indifference. We could say also that it is the defense in depth of this idea of freedom. So that such freedom be protected, the only good antecedent to the will's choice becomes the will itself, and in the name of this supreme value, all rival goods are slaughtered.

This larger view is detailed by Manent, especially in its political connections. It has also been evoked by Iris Murdoch, when, almost forty years ago, she described the man of "modern moral philosophy." She says of modern philosophers in *The Sovereignty of Good* that "although they constantly talk of freedom they rarely talk of love."[8] The understanding of the self this predilection betrays is a function of the freedom of indifference. Murdoch is interested especially in the divorce of freedom so understood from reason.[9] Reason is supposed to be public and objective; will is personal, private, and unbound by any objective values. Rather, this freedom is creative of value: "judgments of value depend upon the will and choice of the individual."[10] "Goodness is not an object of insight or knowledge, it is a function of the will."[11]

---

[8] Iris Murdoch, "The Idea of Perfection," in *The Sovereignty of Good* (New York: Schocken Books, 1970), 2. This essay first appeared in 1964.

[9] Ibid., 5. See Manent on Max Weber, *City of God,* 75.

[10] Murdoch, "The Idea of Perfection," 3.

[11] Ibid., 4.

Reason, which beholds the world, can have nothing to do with freedom, because a value-laden world antecedent to our choice and decision can have nothing to do with it. "If the will is to be totally free the world it moves in must be devoid of normative characteristics."[12] So, looking out into the world, "there is nothing morally to see."[13] The reasons for acting must themselves be freely chosen, and this is what freedom consists in.[14] Isolated not only from reason and reasoned belief, the will is also isolated from feelings and emotion, the harbingers of an objective good independent of the self.[15] The person just is will, "the empty choosing will."[16]

According to the contrary view Murdoch points us to, the will is rather obedient to the good than creator of it.[17] "Freedom is not the sudden jumping of the isolated will in and out of an impersonal logical complex, it is a function of the progressive attempt to see a particular object clearly."[18] Not only is the modern view contrary to our moral experience carefully observed, but it depends on a false antinomy between total freedom and total determinism.[19] And even so, the total freedom it wants seems always on the verge of tipping into its opposite, since a reasonless choice suggests the irrationalism of fatalism.

In a memorable characterization of the modern view, Murdoch reminds us of the capitalist and consumerist society the view is suited to:

> morality is assimilated to a visit to a shop. I enter the shop in a condition of totally responsible freedom, I objectively estimate the features of the goods, and I choose. The greater my objectivity and discrimination the larger the number of products from which I can select.[20]

---

12 Ibid., 42.
13 Ibid., 35.
14 Ibid.
15 Ibid., 8.
16 Ibid., 35.
17 Ibid., 40.
18 Ibid., 23.
19 Ibid., 36.
20 Ibid., 8.

Now, what would happen when the shop items include such things as are involved with life promises, such things as married and family life, or indeed, any life that is worth a life? What happens is that we get the sociological distinction between self and role. This expression of the idea of freedom as freedom of indifference is all the more powerful, moreover, for being divorced from an explicit construction of the history of the idea of freedom or even of philosophy generally. ▪▪

::: *chapter ten*
::: Role Theory and Promising

THIS CHAPTER BEGINS with the psycho-sociological idea of a role, and then takes up two answers as to what the self is where all our interests and actions, obligations and bonds, are absorbed into various roles. Third, we ask whether promises are in or outside roles. Last, there is a word about roles and Kierkegaard's aesthetic self.

It is common today, and not just in departments of sociology, to speak of a person's function or role and distinguish the person from his social roles. This distinction was first introduced into psychology by George Herbert Mead in the 1920s by way of a metaphor from the stage. We are to think of president of the company or mayor of the city or assembly line worker as "roles," related to the person as is the role of Hamlet to Laurence Olivier. We are to think of priest, or father, or mother, son, daughter, in the same way. As T. R. Sarbin writes:

> In general, the term "role" continues to be used to represent the behavior expected of the occupant of a given position or status. Thus, following the implications of the dramaturgic metaphor, an actor assigned to the position (or part) of Hamlet is expected to enact the role of Hamlet, the role being characterized by certain actions and qualities. A person who is assigned to the position of clergyman (or who elects to be placed in such a position

in the social structure) is similarly expected to enact the *role* of clergyman characterized by certain typical actions and qualities.[1]

The metaphor becomes a technical term: "role" means "expected behavior," and playing the role means "enacting expected behavior." And the "audience" is the society, or subsection of the society, on whom the role enactment has an impact. The playwright? Once again, the society, the others before whom and for whom the role is enacted, and who prescribe the relevant expectations.

If "role" is expected behavior, what is "self"? Sarbin:

> the self may be defined as the residue of a human being's transactions with object and event, including other people. These residues are the referents for the symbol *I*.[2]

But then, where all transactions with object, event, and other are role-governed, the "self" is just the residue of previous role-enactments. Again, as R. H. Turner would have it, the self-conception of the individual is a matter of an identification of the self with certain roles.[3] Congruence between self and role, an important variable in predicting adequate role-enactment, is therefore really just a matter of congruence of previous and contemporary roles.

In this light, there are two answers to what the self is. The first answer is that, apart from any residue of roles whatsoever, the self as such disappears, and becomes a sort of dimensionless point, to which various role-vectors are attached; the self is a purely passive, wholly indeterminate and to be determined, with no content outside of the roles taken on. Or, where there is some content to the self in comparison with a role, it is the content of a previous role considered vis-à-vis the content of some new role. As it were, once we have played Hamlet, and gotten used to it, when we shift to Richard II, some parts of this new role are easy, and some are hard.

---

[1] Theodore R. Sarbin, "Role, Psychological Aspects," in *International Encyclopedia of the Social Sciences* (New York: Macmillan, 1968), 13:546b.

[2] Ibid., 13:550b.

[3] Ralph H. Turner, "Role, Sociological Aspects," in *International Encyclopedia of the Social Sciences* (New York: Macmillan, 1968), 13:556a.

Strip away the roles of husband, father, son, brother; strip away the roles of accountant, bowler, and Elk and so on, and what is left of George? An empty, vacuous container. Or on the other hand, you might privilege one of your roles, identify with it as your self. And then you—really, one of your roles—will stand in judgment over against the expectations of the other roles. But it seems always possible in principle to recover my pure self, unalloyed by role. And then how can there be judgment?

On the other hand, we might think there is something missing in the above discussion of role and self, implied but not named, where Turner speaks of the identification of self and role. For this identification takes place by means of a free act. So, freedom is the missing link between self and role, or rather, it is the self. And this is the second answer to the question of what the self is. We need not conceive of the person as an absolutely featureless substrate of societal roles. The one feature of the self-defining self is freedom. The "substrate" is a free self, a self-defining self. The self is a pure freedom anterior to, transcendent to, all roles. Transcendent to role, it transcends all values. Judgments of values define roles, and my judgments of value belong to roles. This is a freedom for which nothing can be valuable prior to a choice of roles. This is Murdoch's "empty choosing will." It is freedom as the freedom of indifference, of which Pinckaers speaks.

According to Manent, both of these answers as to what the self is are entertained by modern consciousness at once. Modern consciousness can be defined by the effort to keep both notions in play together, and man is therefore both wholly passive and autonomously and creatively active.[4] Freedom of will in the Christian medieval sense is denied so that we can be objects of science, a science that knows no finalities or ends, a science that can therefore not impede us in the free pursuit of our desires as both classical thought and Christianity pretended to do in the name of goods both natural and supernatural.

---

[4] Manent, *The City of Man*, 78, 140, 156. This is the paradox of sociology: for it to be a science, Durkheim makes man wholly determined and passive; but if there are no ends and no natural motives toward ends, values must be created, and this is Weber.

Now, on what side of the distinction between self and role is the obligation to keep promises? That is, the promise of marriage till death do us part—is that on the side of the self, does it belong to the self, or does it rather belong to the role of husband or wife, to which the self in its untrammeled freedom of indifference is transcendent? The modern sensibility inclines to the second answer. This means that marriage is, in fact, not at all what it used to be. Part of the idea of marriage was that one could not go back. But today, one certainly can go back, back out, so as to go forward and "get on with life." The freedom to back out, and go forward without baggage, is an implied condition in modern marriage.

The older sensibility, expressed in this modern idiom of roles, would observe that some roles can be the roles they are only if they cannot be put off. That is, some roles have a sort of stability built into them. If a man stops being a plumber, and starts being an engineer, he has not failed in plumbing, and he has not failed in his humanity. But suppose a man stops being a priest; he throws it over and gets married. Why is that thought to be—or why was that thought to be—something morally significant? Presumably, it is because built into the idea of "being a priest" is the idea of a certain permanence. And indeed, the "role" of the priesthood is not entered into without a promise. The promise is not in the role but rather links the self to the role. So, being a priest includes the idea of fidelity to being a priest. But nobody promises to be a plumber. A plumber does not have to promise to be a plumber for life in order to fix your sink.

But someone might say that, No, promise keeping isn't something on the side of the person, on the side of the self; it is on the side of the role. Part of the role of priest, or of married man, is that there is a promise built into it. But the role remains radically detachable from the person. If I am a priest, for as long as I am a priest, I keep my priestly promises—keeping promises (not to get married, to pray, etc.) is something within priesthood. But if I put down the role, then there is no longer any question of my keeping my priestly promises. On this view, it is a mistake to think that the *person* promises to be a priest. No, persons are always free with respect to roles. Promising is within a role, not before it.

But of course, that will not do: you are not a celibate priest until you promise celibacy, just like you are not a married man until you promise to be one. Promising does belong to the person, not to the role. And so, failure to keep the role says something about the person.

Perhaps someone will say that no one in fact argues in the above way when they leave the priesthood.[5] Marriage, however, has certainly been reconceived along the above lines, and there is great difference between this reconceived version and the traditional view of marriage. If John is a married man, what are the expectations? That he not have sexual relations with someone who is not his wife? Yes, that is still expected. That he not divorce his wife? That is so only for the traditional view. The consent that establishes marriage, St. Thomas says, is a consent "to an everlasting bond, else it would make no marriage."[6] Promising is on the side of the person, and perpetuity constitutes the role; it is one of the goods embraced by the promise. For moderns, on the other hand, you are bound by your marriage promises—as long as you stay married. The promises are all within the role, to which freedom is always transcendent. There can be no promise always to be bound by promises—the couple can split up; that is, they can lay aside the roles of husband and wife. That was the point of devising a two-tiered marriage law in Louisiana some years back—a marriage that was as easily left as entered into and recognized as such, and a marriage more like traditional marriage.[7]

When Kierkegaard wrote *Either/Or*, he proposed a choice between the aesthetic life and the ethical life, where the ethical life is paradigmatically represented by the married life. Now, more than 150 years later, the aesthetic life has colonized marriage; marriage

---

5 Even so, talk of a temporary priesthood of thirty years ago has helped destabilize the idea of priesthood as constituted in part by the permanence of the subjective resolve to be and remain a priest.

6 *Summa theologiae*, Suppl. Q. 49, a. 1, ad 4.

7 See David Blankenhorn, "I Do?" *First Things* 77 (November 1997): 14–15, and, more generally, Christopher Wolfe, "The Marriage of Your Choice," *First Things* 50 (February 1995): 37–41.

has been aestheticized. Marriage is no longer something that, once taken up, cannot be put down, but something that we take up and can in principle put down for the most trivial of reasons. It is one more diversion available to a consciousness hungry for experiences, one more possible entertainment for the always transcending, never to be determined freedom of the spouses. Were Kierkegaard writing today, it is hard to know what he could choose as a contrast to the aesthetic life, the foil against which to appreciate it. Increasingly, it seems that all modern lives are now lived within the aesthetic life. This is a life where freedom of indifference is supreme, before which all good things can be shattered and broken.

Let us consider again. Are wife and husband, priest and nun, "roles" in the same sense as are doctor, lawyer, teacher, and are these latter "roles" in the same sense as baker, salesman, or welder? Arguably not. These last roles are constituted by skills, not moral habits; nor are they entered into by a promise. The ones in the second group count as what we used to call the "professions." They seem to bear in themselves some expectation of moral insight and choice. They were understood to have a promise built into them. For doctors, it is the Hippocratic Oath; for a lawyer, it is adherence to a state bar's code of legal ethical practices. And although one does not promise to practice these professions for life, they are commonly associated with lifelong careers in the profession. Even so, while it is no shame to cease practicing a profession, upon occasion and at great need, a retired doctor has once again to start doctoring.

But what of the first set of roles? These are yet more central to the person, to the ensemble of moral beliefs and choices constitutive of the person. Of all roles, they are, or should be, constitutive of the person. If what we mean by the "person" is what the human agent has made of himself in his morally significant choices and promises, then these last roles are not at all something outside of or adventitious to the person. We could say that here there is, and we want there to be, a lasting residue from some "roles."

But then, if wife, husband, priest, nun are roles constitutive of the person, to ask whether one's human fulfillment, or self-realization as a person, goes beyond or is hindered by discharging these roles is a bogus question.

A self that puts on and takes off roles at will is an aesthetic self. Speaking through Judge William in *Either/Or*, the character who represents the ethical stage of life, Kierkegaard suggests that the remedy to the attenuated and disconnected and abstracted self produced by romanticism's exaltation of the freedom of indifference is a choice of choice. If we choose to choose, then the familiar ethical determination of life will be restored to us.[8] Upon reflection, however, this solution seems to remain too beholden to the freedom of indifference. Transcendence is recognized, and that is certainly correct, but it has been emptied out, denaturalized. It orbits too high above the earth. A freedom as empty and formal as Kant's is made by Kierkegaard to produce ethically weighty goods. This is a good trick. But it is in tension with the appreciation of marriage, as earthly a good as we can find, that the Judge in fact presses home. Kierkegaard's real solution to the problem of the aesthetic life, to the problem of freedom of indifference, is in fact his appeal to Christianity. His real solution is an evocation of the goods that Christianity offers. It is to that topic we must turn.

---

[8] Søren Kierkegaard, *Either/Or*, vol. 2, trans. Walter Lowrie, revised by Howard A. Johnson (Princeton, NJ: Princeton University Press, 1971), 170–73.

chapter eleven

Life Promises and the Waning of Christianity

A SECOND EXPLANATION for the difficulty we face today in making life-promises is the waning of the religious influence of Christianity. Although we did not remark it when quoting him, Nietzsche noted that promising, at least serious and important promising, is of old something religious. "Man could never do without blood, torture, and sacrifices when he felt the need to create a memory for himself," he writes; "the cruelest rites of all the religious cults (and all religions are at the deepest level systems of cruelties)—all this has its origin in the instinct that realized that pain is the most powerful aid to mnemonics." Setting aside the invitation Nietzsche sets up for us to think that religious people conceal from themselves the connection of religion and pain, we may take his point. In any case, promising and the gods, promising and God, are related. Where God has been banished as long ago were the gods, what then of promising?

In this chapter, we take religion first as a stick and then as a carrot relative to promises. Then there are two other issues connected with religion and promising, the anticipation of our death and preparation for promising.

As Nietzsche reports it, the threat of retribution in this life or the next at the hand of the gods made the promise trustworthy. Absent such a guarantee, should we trust the word of one who makes a serious promise? Absent such a guarantee, should we trust ourselves to make a serious promise? That is, is it reasonable? Hobbes says that there is nothing so frail as a man's word:

> The force of words being (as I have formerly noted) too weak to hold men to the performance of their covenants, there are in man's nature but two imaginable helps to strengthen it. And those are either a fear of the consequence of breaking their word, or a glory or pride in appearing not to need to break it. This latter is a generosity too rarely found to be presumed on, especially in the pursuers of wealth, command, or sensual pleasure, which are the greatest part of mankind. The passion to be reckoned upon is fear; whereof there be two very general objects: one, the power of spirits invisible; the other, the power of those men they shall therein offend. Of these two, though the former be the greater in power, yet the fear of the latter is commonly the greater fear.[1]

If the one who promises is not Nietzsche's noble man, who will keep his word for glory, we are left with the state or God. Religion provides a stick with which to ensure the keeping of promises, as also the truth of what is attested under oath. For all swearing was a swearing before God and by God, and the point was that God should requite me if I did not speak the truth. Hobbes intimates that, in fact, most men live a sort of practical atheism. There remains the state, and only the state, to make promises binding.

Hobbes considers religion as providing a (mostly ineffectual) stick and no carrot. For many atheists and materialists, if not Hobbes, religion turns out to be a sort of ersatz state.[2] It provides cheap comfort where else there would have to be expensive state welfare. More fundamentally, by its imagination of an All-Seeing and All-Powerful One who nonetheless approves the property arrangements peculiar to technologically sophisticated modern political economies, it keeps the servants from stealing the spoons and middle managers from embezzling company accounts.

---

[1] *Leviathan* I, xiv, 31; 94.

[2] I do not mean here to settle the question of Hobbes's atheism, but hope the reader will grant that in general materialists keep company with atheists.

For those who see, on the other hand, for those who understand that it is their common alienation of natural right to the sovereign that constructs the only power really transcendent to the individual, namely, the state, it is the state alone that guarantees contracts. This guarantee, recall, rests strictly on the capacity of the state to find and prosecute promise breakers. If my only concern is to have as much as I can of goods and the means to other goods, it must remain rational to cheat when I know that the constable is at the other end of the block or that the Securities and Exchange Commission is understaffed and underfunded. That is, my alienation of natural right can never be irrevocable. Hobbes recognizes this when he recognizes the right of condemned men to try to escape their punishment.[3] Max Scheler has this to say about the problem:

> every contract presupposes a common standard incumbent upon both contracting parties, and this standard can only derive from a third party *"in whose eyes"* the contract is binding or not binding.[4]

Could this third party be the Hobbesian state? By no means. According to Scheler, our contract cannot establish the authority by which our contracts are to be kept. The third party, the guarantor superior to both, must already be there.

For Platonists like Murdoch, the Good can serve in the role of guarantor of promises and contracts, for it is something independent of both me and you, and is morally authoritative, prior to our choices.[5] For Christians, it is God who is this authority.

Even so, not enough has been said. The above comparison of God to the state in relation to obligation and promising sins by making the difference between God and Leviathan seem to be that between the true and the false Bully. This is to stay on Hobbes's

---

[3] *Leviathan* I, xiv, 29; 93: "no man can transfer or lay aside his right to save himself from death, wounds, and imprisonment, the avoiding whereof is the only end of laying down any right."

[4] Max Scheler, "Christian Love and the 20th Century," in *On the Eternal in Man*, trans. Bernard Noble (New York: Harper, 1960), 5.

[5] Iris Murdoch, "The Idea of Perfection," in *The Sovereignty of Good* (New York: Schocken Books, 1970), 2. This essay first appeared in 1964.

ground. We must by no means equate the authority Scheler speaks of with Hobbesian power. Moral obligation is not physical restraint. So, it is not just that on our account the stick is to be replaced by the carrot.[6] To be sure, this is a central difference between ancient and modern moral philosophy.[7] But it will not be enough to replace the stick of Hobbesian force with the carrot of what man as Hobbes imagines him wants and would say is good. Rather, we must see that the carrot, the intelligible good, is a good of an altogether different order than what Leviathan threatens to deprive us of.

In this way, the Christian religion contributes more than the threat of punishment to the keeping of promises. It contributes the threat of damnation. Which is to say, it contributes the hope of heaven. For the threat of damnation is not just any old painful state of affairs contrary to our will; it is the loss of heaven, the loss of God, and all the things that participate in God. And life promises were immediately connected with this good. Of old, for instance, marriage was styled a holy thing, a religious good, even, a sacrament, which is to say a participation in the life of God now. More specifically, the married state was a Christian state, modeling the relation between Christ and his Church, imitating the Holy Family, and bringing forth children created in the image of God. All the more was wrecking marriage worthy of retribution, but then, all the more attractive were the goods bound up in it. If obligation derives chiefly from the good promised, then here were very great goods to bind a man and a woman in love and intelligent desire.

I am far from gainsaying the power of the stick to motivate, and to keep people to their word. It may be risky to trust a (modern) man who has never been frightened by the prospect of hell. But we must be careful thinkers here. If we make that the main thing, then we are with Hobbes, and as religious thinkers will have included all things under the sway of a celestial Leviathan. We must weigh whether it is fear or love that is the chief and ruling and informing

---

6 See Thomas S. Hibbs, *Virtue's Splendor: Wisdom, Prudence and the Human Good* (New York: Fordham University Press, 2001), 68.

7 Pierre Manent, *The City of Man,* trans. Marc A. LePain (Princeton, NJ: Princeton University Press, 1998), 43–44, 47–48.

passion. St. Thomas gives us the most cogent reasons for staying faithful to love, and so to the good:

> There is no other passion of the soul that does not presuppose love of some kind. The reason is that every other passion of the soul implies either movement toward something, or rest in something. Now every movement toward something, or rest in something, arises from some kinship or aptness to that thing; and in this does love consist.[8]

We meet again the "kinship" or "aptness" that St. Thomas calls *complacentia* in the good, which is love itself most formally taken and the fundamental bond of lover to beloved, the original "obligation."

We have, moreover, to attend to the kind of good that Christianity is concerned with. All goods of the body are ordained to goods of the soul;[9] moreover:

> the spiritual good is greater than the bodily good, and more enjoyable, and the sign of this is that men abstain even from the greatest bodily pleasures in order not to lose honor, which is an intelligible good.[10]

And of course, the good actually ordained for man is the infinitely intelligible good, the uncreated good of God himself.

Absent religion, there is lost both the carrot of the traditional, even transcendent, goods of Christian marriage and the goad of eternal punishment for adultery. We return to the good of marriage as apprehended by pre-Christian men or arrive at goods of marriage apprehended by secular men. And if the liberty of indifference is the chief good, trumping all others, then the prospects will not be good for marriage "till death do us part." There is not enough weight here to counterbalance the freedom of indifference, especially where that is identified as the very self itself.

---

[8] *Summa theologiae* I–II, Q. 27, a. 4, c. See his commentary on *The Divine Names*, chapter 4, lectio 9: love "is the first and common root of all appetitive operations"; that is, of desire, joy, and sadness alike.

[9] *Summa theologiae* I–II, Q. 2, a. 5, c.

[10] *Summa theologiae* I–II, Q. 31, a. 5, c.

There is another reason the passing of Christianity makes life promises more difficult. To promise something for life makes us contemplate death. When we marry, we contemplate the death of ourselves and our spouses. Priestly or religious promising also has us look forward to death. If we are a people who cannot face death, as is commonly alleged, then we must also be a people who cannot face promising for life. Now, the passing of Christianity makes it harder for us to keep death daily before our eyes, since we think of it as personal annihilation. It is troublesome and maybe impossible to look at a limit that has nothing beyond it. Christianity lets us look beyond the limit of death, and so look at death itself. But now, we have only the comfort of the unimaginability of such a death. Indeed, when we try to picture to ourselves the annihilation of consciousness, there we are, still picturing it. We show up like Tom Sawyer in the choir loft, looking at our funeral. But what if there is no longer any choir loft from which I can look down on the obsequies, confident I will see something after my funeral is over? If it really is true that I cannot look squarely at death, however, then I cannot really make a life promise. And more and more, it seems, we do not do so in America.

The waning of Christianity enfeebles the capacity to make life promises in yet another way. For some promises, I know beforehand pretty well what I am promising, what I am engaged to do. If I promise to take Aunt Mary to the doctor, this is something I have done many times before. And even the first time, I knew already about doctors, Aunt Mary, and car trips. But there are other promises whose carrying out is not so readily imagined and divined ahead of time. Does anyone really know what he is promising when he marries? There is engagement, but still, the answer is No. We cannot have direct and complete experience of marriage, an insider's experience, as it were, before (our first) marriage, and the witness of our parents and other married people cannot fully substitute for this lack. Part of the adventure of marriage is bound up with this inability to know beforehand exactly what it will take.

Again, some promising is repetitive—I have made such promises before, and know what it is like to have so promised. But marriage—

the first marriage, anyway—is peculiar. I cannot altogether know what it is like to make such a promise for life until I have made it and begun to live it. We cannot practice making a once-for-all promise the way we can practice shooting a twelve-gauge. Of old, the willingness to step where one could not quite imagine oneself being until one was there served as a sort of initiation to personal maturity. Had someone promised—for life—or not? If he had, he had exercised the time-transcending power of man. If not, he remained a child, measuring things by inches and not by leagues, by seconds and not the decades of a man's years.

Now, into this incapacity fully to imagine before what one was doing, and what one was getting into, there stepped the greatest consolation of religion. I speak here of marriage—all the more and more obviously was becoming a priest or monk religiously determined. But marriage, too, the life promise constituting it, could be parasitic on the previous life promise of Christian faith itself. If there is a Power that can help me keep the commandments in both the letter and the spirit, overcome pride, and restrain concupiscence, so that I may hope to celebrate the heavenly nuptials of the Lamb, then I may also have good hope that the wedding feast of today will be no lie, and that the little nuptials of this earth will be successfully concluded in keeping my vows day by day.

The ocean that bore up the ship of the Church could bear up also the small boats of Christian marriage. The tide that carried us to the other shore in the great bark could also buoy up the little barks of our families. When the ocean is drained away, all the vessels are high and dry.

chapter twelve

::::: Life Promises and the
::::: Privatization of Christianity

WHAT WE HAVE CALLED the waning of Christianity is sometimes called secularization. "Secularization" bespeaks the advance of some rational and disenchanting order of science and of man "come of age." If it means people do not go to church like they used to, then the Pacific Northwest is more secular than the rest of the country, and Europe is more secular than America. On the other hand, it might be that where Christianity wanes, some other religions wax. The weakening of the hold of Christianity on western culture is not necessarily the passing of all religious sensibility. Especially, if religion means having a view of what is the first principle of things, then lots of people today accord to "evolution" the place Christians accord to God.[1] Rather than secularization, it is more exact to think in terms of the privatization of Christianity and the Church.

This privatizing is the Enlightenment solution to the West's theologico-political problem. The medieval solutions, as Pierre Manent explains, were first to let the Church rule, then second to

---

[1] Robert Sokolowski, "The Authority of Philosophy in *Fides et ratio*," in *Restoring Faith in Reason*, ed. Laurence Paul Hemming and Susan Frank Parsons (London: SCM Press, 2002), 282: "People may say that the evolution of living things is based on purely accidental mutations, but when they speak more generally about it they attribute to it a providence and a superior intelligence that strongly resembles the Mind *(Nous)* that the Presocratic philosopher Anaxagoras said was part of nature."

try a strict separation of powers, ecclesial and temporal. If the Church (or presbytery) cannot be let to rule, however, and if there is no space outside the city she can be banished to, then the footing on which she can be suffered to remain is that she be relegated to the sphere of "society" as distinct from the public space of public policy. She must be relegated to the sphere of the "private."[2]

The private is the sphere of free opinion, where men's differences over ends cannot lead them to blows, because all the means of public authority have been ceded to a state that is programmatically agnostic about the natural goods of man and his true end. The end of the best of the recognized classical regimes was to foster virtue and the attainment of happiness objectively conceived. The end of the modern state is to provide a civic canopy over the liberty of the citizens to think whatever thoughts they want about their happiness, and to follow in its pursuit whatever they desire, a liberty limited only by a concern not to get in the way of another man's similarly freely chosen but perhaps quite differently oriented path. Modern society as protected by the modern state is ordained to increase the scope of freedom, the freedom of indifference, to be sure, by which we create values, there being no goods antecedent to choice to discover and serve. Within society, state monopoly on power means that persuasion is the only resource within society and its parts to influence behavior.

Now, promising for life in the premodern order was most certainly about goods both natural and supernatural, goods directed to or constitutive of the end of man as ordained by his Maker. Promising of old was ordered to great goods, and keeping these promises was a partial realization of man as virtuous, whether naturally or supernaturally, but in any case as the core element of his happiness now and in the life to come. The modern state that resolutely refuses a position on nature and the good must consequently forbear publicly to foster or positively to sanction such life promises. Like religion, they can be tolerated. But the modern state cannot consistently with its inability to know nature and natural ends make

---

2 Manent, *The City of Man,* 169–70, 177; "Christianity and Democracy," 102–3.

the standard of the Church a public standard. So, there can be no right in the modern state to marry until death part the spouses. That would suppose a view of marriage and of the ends of marriage and of man that it is the compact of the state not to privilege, not so much because of the content of the view, but because it is a view. The state is not to have views, let alone a single authoritative view, on such things. The modern state therefore has no interest in forming men who make and keep life promises. Modern society, for its part, is a cacophony on the subject. Insofar as the state is an advanced political economy wed to a rapidly changing technological infrastructure, moreover, it seems rather to have an interest in the mobility and flexibility of the workforce, even if this occurs at the expense of the stability of marriage and families.

Consequent to the modern state's self-professed ignorance of nature, we see contemporarily not only the countenancing of divorce, but the relinquishment even of the definition of marriage as rooted in the natural distinction of the sexes and as ordered to the procreation of the species. The state has views about safeguarding public health and so can require a blood test prior to issuing a marriage license or forbid marriage within certain degrees of kinship. The state takes steps to head off certain foreseeable results of certain kinds of sexual congress or of sexual congress under certain circumstances. But it is hard for the state to take a view about what sexual congress is for. If we are fast tending to take it that any two people of whatever sex or intention who say they are married are "married," the state does not have the resources to resist this adjustment of language and social reality.[3] The more and more ready assent of the state to changing societal view is entirely consistent with the modern political philosophy's inability to speak of nature or of natural ends. To say nay would be to invoke a standard long renounced by the modern state.

The only voice that does say nay is the voice of the Church. And this she does with perfect propriety, according to the modern

---

3 Further, while polyandry might be thought to have pretty obviously undesirable consequences, it is hard to know on what grounds the State of Utah should resist polygyny.

consciousness, but only as one among many other voices sounding different opinions within the civil conversation of society. What cannot be, however, is that the Church have the stature of a public voice addressed universally to the commonwealth as such. She must perforce have the stature of speaking in a societal voice, which is to say a private voice to those who wish to listen. And as a privatized voice, hers must be one voice among many speaking on the ends of man and what it is good to try to do. Her discourse on promising, and the good of promising for life, and the goods life promises respond to, will be one tract among many. This must have the consequence that the life-promising she still upholds as one of the chief constituents of a good life must often be lost to view.

It will be true, too, that the privatized Church becomes a democratized Church. That is, existing in private space in the bosom of a democratized and egalitarian state, the temptation will be great to think of the Church on the lines of a modern state, where all citizens are equal, where there is rule of law, and where authority depends on the consent of the governed. Here, Manent says, "the decisive question is avoided: Does or does not the church have the right to command me?"[4] So we hear much about baptismal equality, about the rights of the laity, and about consulting the faithful wherever some rule of faith, or sacramental rite, or governance is to be laid down. The relevance of different measures of holiness, of the personal authority of apostolic ministers, and of obedience to the Gospel will be harder and harder to keep focused. Modern man is neither magnanimous nor humble, as Manent says, but he wants to be consulted.[5]

In this way, the voice of the Church tends to fracture and pluralize, and Christianity itself, from the inside, is conceived by Christians to be an association to be made in whatever shape with whatever content those in the association want to make it.

I do not wish to be taken here for pretending that modern democracy does not bring great goods with it or that in any event it

---

[4] "Christianity and Democracy," 113.
[5] Manent, *The City of Man*, 201–2.

is not irresistible.[6] Moreover, we can be glad to forsake the attempt to legislate in favor of the Church if those we live with forsake the attempt to legislate against her. On the other hand, it is naïve not to reckon the cost to Christians of the modern settlement. Goods lose some of their luster where they cannot be publicly acclaimed as universally to be guarded by the commonwealth itself in its concern for the common good. How can these goods be good for me if they are not good for you and do not rule us both?[7] It is not a matter of seeking a "solution" to the problem of how to be Christians and how to situate the Church in the modern age, but of being thoughtful about our prospects.

---

6 Ibid., 160.
7 Manent, *The City of Man,* 180.

chapter thirteen

::: Promises and Christianity

I F WE WANT TO THINK about promises within the context of Christianity, we face a problem of control. Does
anything within Christianity escape the economy of promise and
fulfillment? Abraham, the father of faith, has faith in the promise of
God that God will make of him a great nation in whom all the
nations will be blessed. The covenants between God and the Patri-
archs, God and the people of Israel at Sinai, God and David—what
are these but mutual exchanges of promises? Jesus of Nazareth is the
promised Messiah. Himself, he promises a hundredfold to those
who follow him. He promises that the gates of hell shall not prevail
against his Church. He promises life everlasting to the sister of
Lazarus. He promises paradise to the good thief. He promises forgiveness of sin through the ministry of the apostles. He promises to
return again in glory. On our part, we enter the Church through
baptism, which is not accomplished unless we make our baptismal
promises. "Testament" translates *diathēkē*, which translates *berît*,
"covenant"—or "promise." Things could well have fallen out so that
we would refer to the parts of the Bible as the Old Promise and the
New Promise.[1]

---

[1] For some fine grain, see Dennis J. McCarthy, SJ, *Treaty and Covenant: A Study
in Form in the Ancient Oriental Documents and in the Old Testament*, new ed.
completely rewritten (Rome: Biblical Institute Press, 1978), and Tony W. Cart-
ledge, *Vows in the Hebrew Bible and the Ancient Near East, Journal for the Study
of the Old Testament*, Supplement Series, 147 (Sheffield: JSOT Press, 1992).

The language and practice of making covenants in the Old Testament bears directly on the contention that promising explicitly attaches us to a good whose solicitation we have already felt. For ancient practice, including that reported in the Old Testament and pressed into theological service there, formal establishment of a covenant gives further binding force to an already existing relationship. So to speak, a promise turns out to be a binding recognition of an already existing bond of friendship between persons.

So much can be gathered from the work of Moshe Weinfeld. He reports that the terms for covenants and pacts in the ancient Near East collect in two semantic fields, "oath and commitment on the one hand, grace and friendship on the other."[2] This linguistic fact is common to the Mesopotamian, Syrian, Hebrew, Greek, and Roman literature of treaty making. One undertakes a commitment with an oath, and so strengthens an already existing relationship of friendship, peace, brotherhood, love between the parties.[3] In the Old Testament, covenant relations are thus to be described in terms of steadfast love (ḥesed), faithfulness ('emet), peace, friendship. Further, one maintains a covenant and performs the good by remembering the goodness and faithfulness the other party has done and shown one. Of course, it is not as if the oath or the formal covenant promises add nothing to the already extant state of affairs:

> in spite of our recognized connection between "good/kindness" and "covenant" it should be pointed out that not always do these concepts overlap. N. Glueck has rightly said in regard to *hsd* that: "*hesed* [steadfast love] is the premise and effect of *berïth* [covenant]; it constitutes the very essence of a *berïth* but is not yet a *berïth*, even though there can be no *berïth* without *hesed*."[4]

---

[2] Moshe Weinfeld, "Covenant Terminology in the Ancient Near East and its Influence on the West," *Journal of the American Oriental Society* 93 (1973): 190.

[3] Ibid., 194–96.

[4] Ibid., 192–93. See N. Glueck, *Hesed in the Bible,* trans. Alfred Gottschalk, ed. Elias L. Epstein (Cincinnati: Hebrew Union College Press, 1967), 68.

The good, beholding the good, is essential to a promise but is not yet promising. Dennis McCarthy, speaking of the negotiations leading up to making a covenant in the ancient Near East, comments:

> The negotiations . . . begin regularly with an affirmation that a real though general relationship already exists between the parties. They commonly conclude with a clearer definition of the relationship.[5]

A clearer definition, a greater manifestation, which is good, of the already good relationship—that is what the covenant effects.

So much is to point out what is common between human promising and promising that involves God. There are also special features of the promises God makes to us and we to him to be noted here and in the next chapter. Examining these differences will help us appreciate both our position before God and the nature of promising itself. Notwithstanding the differences, promising is a bridge that holds up across the great chasm between creature and Creator, a most astonishing thing, like faith, Emily Dickinson's Pierless Bridge.

Also, it is a most necessary thing. It must be that our relations with God are structured according to a pattern of promise and fulfillment. From our side, this is a function of the temporality of our agency. The modification of our environment that we effect, the acquisition of virtue we undertake, the disposition of ourselves that we achieve in regard to another, not excluding God, all of these take time, for they all involve passages from potency to act. Such passage is motion. And the measure of motion, one of them, is time. We possess ourselves only in and with time. Promising anticipates our accomplishments, our growth, and our donations of self, including our donations of ourselves to the eternal God. Even more, because God is God, we will want to anticipate our donation of ourselves to him in a promise before we can finish it in fact. We will want to signify the completeness we intend, for more than even every ordinary love, a donation of self to him calls for completeness. We will want to promise the whole of ourselves to him from whom we have received the whole of ourselves, first by creation, and second by the

---

[5] McCarthy, *Treaty and Covenant,* 19.

re-creation of grace and redemption. The response to God we make now cannot be correct, in other words, unless it entails that we want it to be complete, that we would, if we could, anticipate the days of our lives and cast them all as a response back to God. Love wishes to promise itself. It cannot be correct unless it wants to be a promised love. Hans Urs von Balthasar:

> Love can never be content with an act of love performed for the present moment only. It wants to abandon itself, to surrender itself, to entrust itself, to commit itself to love. As a pledge of love, it wants to lay its freedom once and for all at the feet of love. As soon as love is truly awakened, the moment of time is transformed for it into a form of eternity. . . . Hence, every true love has the inner form of a vow: It binds itself to the beloved— and does so out of motives and in the spirit of love. Every participation in the love of God partakes of the nature of a vow.[6]

As we should expect, however, vows or promises to God, including our baptismal promises, differ from ordinary promises in some ways.[7] For instance, God does not have to wait to see whether we will fulfill our promises. He does not have to take our word for it, for the time of our promising and the time of our fulfillment are equally present to him. Eternity encompasses time, as the psalmist notes when he says that in God's book all our days were written "when as yet there was none of them" (Ps 139:16). In our ordinary promising, both parties look forward into a certain indeterminacy and obscurity. For both, the question of how things will play out is real. But this is true only of us, and not God, when we promise something to him.

The most important difference from ordinary promises, perhaps, is that the fulfillment of our promises to God makes for our good, not his.[8] God's good cannot be increased or decreased by anything in the created order, since he is the Creator. Our promises to

---

[6] Hans Urs von Balthasar, *The Christian State of Life,* trans. Sister Mary Frances McCarthy (San Francisco: Ignatius Press, 1983), 38–39. See also 58–65. "A self-surrender that is temporary is not a genuine self-surrender" (61).

[7] Popularly, a vow is a solemn promise, especially of fidelity; religiously, a vow is any promise to God.

[8] *Summa theologiae* II–II, Q. 88, a. 4.

him could be said, as St. Anselm might say, to serve and increase his extrinsic honor; they serve to the manifestation in the created order of his goodness and holiness. Again, the fulfillment of our promises to God may serve him in the sense of accomplishing his purpose for us or for others. But as the fourth preface to the Eucharistic prayer for weekdays says, "you have no need of our praise, yet our desire to thank you is itself your gift; our prayer of thanksgiving adds nothing to your greatness, but helps us grow in your grace."

As an exercise of charity, or as imbued with charity, the fulfillment of our promises is an act of friendship, for charity is friendship with God.[9] In this, keeping our promises to God is like keeping our promises generally. But friendship with God is not natural. Friendship with God depends on his inviting us to share in his own happiness and goodness, to possess it as he possesses it; friendship with God supposes grace and the gift of charity.[10]

That we make the promises we do at baptism therefore evidently presupposes the promise God makes to us and its fulfillment. For our promise is to lead a supernatural life, a life whose principle is grace and whose powers are the theological virtues of faith, hope, and charity, all of which are gifts. The fulfillment of our promise depends on God's fulfillment of his promise to send us the Holy Spirit. Again, our promising before God, to God, evidently presupposes we know and believe the promise God makes to us in Christ; our promises are responses to God's promise, his word.

Because of the relation of creature to Creator, and of grace to nature, things are more radical than is captured by saying that we can only respond to God and that he has the initiative. This is true; but we could say the same of the relation of king and peasant. However we discharge our promises to God, whether with created powers or supernatural virtues, he gives us the wherewithal to do so, and absolutely down to the last penny of our investment. There are analogies in the created order. Spouses support one another in their mutual discharge of promises. A lord may give his vassal the land

---

[9] *Summa theologiae* II–II, Q. 23, a. 1.
[10] *Summa theologiae* II–II, Q. 23, aa. 1 and 2; Q. 24. a. 2.

and equipment with which to fulfill his promise. Even in these cases, however, an agent possesses goods used in fulfilling the promise that were not given him by the one to whom he is promising. But in promising to God, the very freedom with which I make the promise, the act of promising, the discharge of the promise, all these are created things, all are his prior donation, whether of nature or of grace. Our merits are his gifts.   ∷

chapter fourteen

::: God's Promises to Us

W
HY SHOULD GOD MAKE promises to us? I do not
mean to ask in the first place: why does he give us
good things, or make good things, or create anything at all? He creates for the manifestation of his glory, to us, and therefore for our
good, out of generosity. For he does not need to be informed of his
goodness, and so he needs no external manifestation of his glory, nor
can the Creator add to his goodness by creating something that perforce must be a participation of his infinite goodness. Granted that,
still, why does he make promises? Why, from his side, should his
agency and good will toward us have the rhythm of promise and fulfillment? Our temporally extended agency requires time to accomplish anything, and we may well make promises to God. But his
agency is not temporally stretched. It is eternal, included in the simul-
taneous all at once possession of interminable life that eternity is.[1] If
he wishes to give the land to Abraham, why does he not just do it?
Why does he make Abraham wait? If he wishes to raise up a king after
his own heart in the house of David, why does he not simply do it?
Why make the people wait, and while they wait, promise them?

The answer is that it is once again a matter of our good. It is a
matter of how we human beings come to appreciate things. Not only
is our agency temporally distended, but our powers of appreciation
are, too. So, to take an obvious instance, the Last Supper and the

---

[1] See *Summa theologiae* I, Q. 10, a. 1.

Christian Eucharist are both necessary for our appreciation of Calvary. The Supper anticipates and the Eucharist recollects the Cross, which becomes what it is, and possesses the reality it does, only in such re-presencing; the Eucharist lets the Cross and the Supper both be what they want to be, and this takes many Christian altars scattered not only throughout space but through time as well.[2] There is also a prior layer of promise and anticipation in the Old Testament. The anticipation of the Supper and the Eucharist in the Passover meal and Temple sacrifice are necessary for us to appreciate the goods of the Supper and the Eucharist for what they are. The paschal lamb, promise of the Lamb of God who takes away the sin of the world, helps us recognize the Lamb slain before the foundation of the world whom we receive at communion. Just as we have to get many perspectives on a great work of architecture to appreciate it, looking now from here, now from over there, so the events of salvation require many temporal perspectives for their appreciation, and in that way, they become the event they began to be when, as we say, they happened. Promising and prophesying beforehand help provide us the diversity of perspective we need to appreciate events.

The fact that things anticipated are more appreciated is true of promising itself. That is, God's promises are themselves objects of previous promisings. There is a history of promising, a succession of covenants, a trajectory necessary for us to appreciate the end of the history justly and with due admiration. God says to Abraham at Genesis 17:7, "I will establish my covenant between me and you and your descendents." And so the Lord proceeds to do, making the covenant of circumcision, promising both the land and an heir of his own flesh from Sarah. But there has already been the covenant of Genesis 15, promising descendants as numerous as the stars of the heavens and the land. And this covenant is but to strengthen Abraham's faith in the original promises of chapter 12. The promise of God founds the relation, is looked back on within the relation, is renewed and

---

[2] See on this Robert Sokolowski, *Eucharistic Presence: A Study in the Theology of Disclosure* (Washington, DC: Catholic University of America Press, 1994), 28–30; and see chapter 8, "The Time of the Eucharist."

renewed again. The Lord fulfills the promise he makes to Moses at the burning bush (Ex 3), so that he may promise again at Sinai (Ex 19–24), and so that Sinai may be renewed in the plains of Moab (Dt 29). Most remarkably, there is the explicit promise through Jeremiah of a covenant, a final covenant, a covenant written not on tablets but on the heart (31:33). Receiving the promise of God requires anticipation, contemplation, growth on our part. It is not the work of a day, for the reason that we, individually and as the people of God, cannot be the work of a day. It is just not in our nature that things could be otherwise, and God respects the natures he makes.

In the second place, it is perhaps worthwhile to point out that God could not promise except to agents like us. There are two reasons for this. The duration proper to the three Persons of the Trinity is that of eternity, where there is no past and no future.[3] Promising, however, requires that at least one of the parties be in time and have a future that is outside of past and present. We temporally extended creatures can make a promise to the eternal God. The eternal God can make a promise to us temporal creatures. But the eternal Father cannot promise anything to the eternal Son or vice versa. Promising requires a temporal distance between the promise and the fulfillment, and there is no such thing within the duration proper to God. For a similar reason, there is not enough distension for a divine promise to angels. Angelic knowledge, and the self-determination of angelic freedom all in a moment, are too densely concentrated, as it were, for there to be a role for promising in their salvation.[4]

Additionally, promising also requires a distinction of wills between the one promising and the one who receives the promise. But in the Trinity, all things are common except the Persons themselves. They are not distinct according to nature or what follows from nature. Now, will is the appetite that pertains to intellectual nature. The three Persons have one will. They do not make promises to one another.

In the third place, if God promises us something, it will similarly be as when we promise him, that the thing promised is for our

---

[3] *Summa theologiae* I, Q. 10, a. 1.

[4] See, for example, *Summa theologiae* I, Q. 62, a. 5.

good and not for his. It can be good for us both as to what is promised and as to the certain expectation we may have that he will give us the good thing promised. And there will be as well the good of the display of all this, the display of the divine goodness, of the good promised, and of the certainty of hope. But, evidently, God will not promise for the stability of his will. The divine will, one with the divine being, is immutable.[5] And because of the divine eternity, in the same eternal moment in which he promises, he fulfills the promise. Our hearing of the promise and our receipt of its fulfillment may be temporally distinct, but the divine action that produces temporally distinct effects is eternally one.

Of course, whatever God gives to any creature can be nothing but a participated likeness of him. That is what the creature itself is. There is no good other than and not already included in the infinite Good. In this way, the divine will can love nothing except the divine goodness, and all that he wills is willed in his willing of his own goodness, for all things are but imitations of it. That he therefore cannot want anything or give anything except what is a participation of himself is a function of the infinity of his goodness and bespeaks a generosity, the generosity of creation, than which we could conceive no greater, were it not for revelation. For revelation does give us to think a greater generosity, where, according to the Bible, God gives not just participations of himself or likenesses of himself, but himself. The form of the covenant ceremonies in the Old Testament shows this in a striking way.

Exodus 24 is especially noteworthy in this respect. Moses receives and writes the words of the commandments of the Lord. Then, we read:

> he rose early in the morning, and he built an altar at the foot of the mountain, and twelve pillars according to the twelve tribes of Israel. And he sent young men of the people of Israel, who offered burnt offerings and sacrificed peace offerings of oxen to the Lord. And Moses took half of the blood and put it in basins, and half of

---

[5] *Summa theologiae* I, Q. 19, a. 7.

the blood he threw against the altar. Then he took the book of the covenant, and read it in the hearing of the people; and they said, "All that the Lord has spoken we will do, and we will be obedient." And Moses took the blood and threw it upon the people, and said, "Behold the blood of the covenant which the Lord has made with you in accordance with all these words." (vv. 4–8)

Blood is life, the seat of life, as also the Bible says quite clearly (Gen 9:4, Lev 17:11). Therefore, to share in blood—half thrown on the altar, God's place, and half on the people—signifies communion of life, a common life. And a common life, as Aristotle points out, is what is most characteristic of friends. Moreover, this is a life that is properly personal, rational, *logikos,* for between the two pourings of the blood, as it were, enclosed by the two pourings, there is the reading of the ordinances of the Lord. The common life means a common mind, a common will and love. In this sense, the most important fulfillment of the covenant occurs just according as the people keep the words and so stay in communion of one mind and one heart with God.

chapter fifteen

Surety for God's Promises to Us

THERE IS A FOURTH ISSUE in addition to the three raised in the previous chapter. The question of surety raises special questions when the promise is God's promise. For it would seem impossible that we should need any surety that God will fulfill his promise. Our confidence that he will be faithful to his promise must be a confidence greater than we have in any other agent. For he is omnipotent and can do all things, whatever he wills. And his veracity is absolute; he can neither deceive nor be deceived. Such confidence as God warrants, therefore, precludes asking for or even wanting a surety. Even to ask for a surety, even to ask him to swear as men swear, mistakes the position of God. As the Letter to the Hebrews remarks, "men indeed swear by a greater than themselves" (6:16). But what is greater than God? So, in Isaiah 45:23, God swears by himself that he will save Israel. His trustworthiness cannot be shored up by anything outside it. God is not threatened by any impediment to his agency and can fear nothing. He cannot be made or moved by anything outside himself to do anything, and it is only for the sake of himself, his "name," that he honors his promise and saves (e.g., Is 48:9–11; Jer 14:21; Ez 20:22, 44; 36:21–22; cf. Ex 32:11–14).

If God has promised, then, there is no surety needed nor fittingly asked for. Even so, what may not fittingly be asked for can graciously be given. After the Flood, the Lord condescends to show Noah that He has fashioned a guarantee for the divine memory:

> I set my bow in the cloud, and it shall be a sign of the covenant
> between me and the earth. When I bring clouds over the earth
> and the bow is seen in the clouds, I will remember my covenant
> which is between me and you and every living creature of all
> flesh; and the waters shall never again become a flood to destroy
> all flesh. When the bow is in the clouds I will look upon it and
> remember. (Gen 9:13–16)

We saw earlier that Nietzsche makes memory the product of blood
and pain. The Lord God makes use of an altogether different kind
of *aide-de-mémoire*, the beautiful bow, whose arc outlines something
of the transcendence of God himself, and is calculated to reassure
Noah as to the capaciousness and accuracy of the divine memory.

The question of surety returns, however, in another way for the
divine promises. For how are we confident in the first place that he
has indeed promised? While we cannot doubt his ability to fulfill
his promises or the veracity of his speech, we may well be tempted
to doubt that he is speaking and making a promise at all. When a
man makes us a promise, we may doubt its fulfillment, or even
doubt whether he intends sincerely to fulfill it. But we do not doubt
he is saying "I promise" to us when he is saying it. How do we know
God promises? How do we know the promises of God? The story of
Gideon moves within this logic. "If now I have found favor with
thee, then show me a sign that it is thou who speakest with me" (Jgs
6:17). Arguably, the subsequent requests for a sign—as for the dew
on the fleece—are of the same nature. Gideon asks for a sign so that
he can be sure not that the Lord can do what he says he will do, but
that it is really the Lord who is promising and that he is really hearing a divine promise.

How do we know the promises of God? We will ask this question all the more urgently as it seems that his promises are not fulfilled. If the Lord promised, his promise will certainly be fulfilled.
But, if there is no fulfillment, then he never promised. This is the
argument in play in Psalm 77, for instance. The psalmist remembers
past mighty deeds for consolation in the present, but the question
arises whether God has "forgotten to be gracious," whether his

promises are "at an end for all time" (vv. 8, 9). If we remain in our misery, then the promise is no more; there has been no promise.

Ghislain Lafont points to the figure of Job. Job's experience seems to be that of a God who has broken his promise. God was supposed to punish the wicked and reward the just, and he has not done it. How can he be trusted? An unreliable God, however, is not God. For the psalmist, doubt about the content of the divine promise becomes doubt about its existence. Likewise, doubt about the nature of God turns to doubt of his existence. For his part, Job learns it is wrong to ask how it is that God can be trusted. It is wrong to put God to the test of man's questions and expectations. And yet, in some fashion, the Lord does offer Job some surety. As it were, when the Lord arrives at the end of the story to answer Job, he refuses any surety *within* the world, but offers the surety of the whole of creation itself. Leviathan and Behemoth, pieces of creation put on display when the Lord speaks from the whirlwind, serve to evoke the immeasurable breadth and awesomeness of the whole of creation. And this whole in turn witnesses to the unfathomability of a divine transcendence that, in Lafont's word, is "incontestable."[1] It cannot be put to the test because there is no witness *(testis)* to it not created by it. So, we can say, it is not the created whole that is offered as surety, but the very creating of God. And this is to say that the Lord offers Himself, alone, for surety, since the act of creation is not distinct from Him.[2] To the display of creation and the evocation of the creative act, Job submits, and, it is important to note, the Lord then fulfills his promise, and in terms Job can understand—land, family, wealth.

The idea of creation as surety for God's promises plays an important role in the theology of the Old Testament, or we might better say, in coming to confess God as creator. So to speak, the Old Testament argument proceeds in this wise: God is trustworthy, and Israel can trust him to fulfill his promises to redeem her, only if he

---

[1] Ghislain Lafont, *God, Time, and Being,* trans. Leonard Maluf (Petersham, MA: Saint Bede's Publications, 1992), 197–98.

[2] *Summa theologiae* I, Q. 45, a. 3, ad 1.

is Creator. Psalm 74, for instance, a lament over the despoiling of the Temple, invokes the surety of God as creator; creation is the first of his saving works, the stronger ground upon which we can stand even if the Temple is desecrated. This link is especially important in Deutero-Isaiah. Consider Isaiah 51:9–11:

> Awake, awake, put on strength,
> O arm of the Lord;
> awake as in days of old,
> the generations of long ago.
> Was it not thou that didst cut Rahab in pieces,
> that didst pierce the dragon?
>
> Was it not thou that didst dry up the sea,
> the waters of the great deep;
> that didst make the depths of the sea a way
> for the redeemed to pass over?
>
> And the ransomed of the Lord shall return,
> and come to Zion with singing;
> everlasting joy shall be upon their heads;
> they shall obtain joy and gladness,
> and sorrow and sighing shall flee away.

The first and second verses are joined literarily by the image of the sea as chaos. In the second, the chaos of the sea is rendered a path for the exodus of Israel from Egypt. In the first, creation is described as victory over the sea monster. Both of these acts, then, creation and the historical liberation of Israel, are acts of one transcendent power. And by this same power, according to the third stanza, Israel will return from Babylon.[3]

In this light, then, are the great creation texts of Genesis to be read. The assertion of God as Creator explains why his guarantee of the history of Israel is sure; creation functions as the guarantee, the surety, of the fulfillment of the promise, any delay to the contrary notwithstanding.

---

[3] See Isaiah 45:9–13, 18–25.

The delay of the fulfillment of the promise leads to a greater appreciation of God as Creator, therefore. Also, it leads to a better appreciation of just what it is that God is offering, of what the content of the promise is. The apparent nonfulfillment of the covenant is a part of the education of Israel. One feels this happening in Psalm 73. Punishment and reward are not meted out in this life according to the promise of Deuteronomy; therefore, perhaps there is another life, and the magnitude of what God offers us comes more to light: "My flesh and my heart fail, but God is the strength of my heart and my portion for ever. . . . [F]or me it is good to be near God" (Ps 73:26, 28).

Sometimes, however, the apparent nonfulfillment of prior promise leaves what can be described only as a sort of open wound. Psalm 89 measures the end of Judah's kingly line against the clearest promises given to David. It, too, invokes God as creator in vv. 9–10, where the defeat of chaos in the person of the monster Rahab is evoked. Even so and notwithstanding, the psalm ends in bewilderment: "Lord, where is thy steadfast love of old, which by thy faithfulness thou didst swear to David?" (v. 49).

The New Testament will walk into this open space of frustrated Davidic promise and Messianic expectation, and declare a fulfillment of divine promise in Jesus of Nazareth. However, Jesus' rearticulation of the content of God's promises, Lafont notes, was challenging:

> it is important to see clearly that his Messianic word, like every other word of God in the preceding history, offered a dilemma of attraction and repulsion: however radiant may have been the figure of Jesus or his power as a wonder worker, which accredited his message, the latter was nonetheless extremely onerous, and at the limit of the tolerable. The fact is that Jesus took a position with respect to the Mosaic law that was at the same time one of liberty and one of respect. It was hardly evident how this position should be interpreted. One would have to have understood that the fulfillment of the Law of Moses in the Kingdom passed through a transformation whose authority was guaranteed by the word of Jesus alone.[4]

---

[4] Lafont, *God, Time, and Being,* 227–28.

We will see later how Jesus himself meets the issue of offering surety. We know of course that this must be a matter of his death and resurrection. For the present, it will be good to connect our topic with the theological tracts on revelation and faith. The question of surety for God's promises is analogous to the question of how the "signs of credibility" are related to faith.

In the first place, the signs—just in their character as pointing to divine agency, and not as illustrative of what the product of that agency is or of what the divine working is leading up to—give no apodictic proof that God is revealing. So, also, no sign or surety can give proof that God is promising. Were there proof that God is revealing, we should not embrace what is revealed freely, in faith. And were there proof that God is promising, we should not embrace what is promised freely, in hope. And in both cases, should we ask for such proof, we should be measuring the divine veracity by something outside it, which is a denial of the divine transcendence and tantamount to blasphemy. The recourse to the fact of creation in the context of asking about God's credibility registers the impropriety of seeking a sign proving that God has made a promise, that is, it points us to the lesson of Job.

But in the second place, just as the signs of credibility make acceptance of the fact that he is speaking, and the acceptance of what he says when he speaks, something reasonable, so also does the surety God offers make hope in his promises reasonable. He does enough so that we may have some rest from the importunate questions of a mind that is not satisfied except by sight. This is surety such as he gives to Moses or to Gideon.

That is, a little more at length, things turn out with faith as follows. When I believe both that God reveals and what he reveals, I believe on the sole ground that he is revealing. But suppose someone asks me, Why do you believe—why do you think it reasonable? Then I may point to some "extrinsic sign of credibility" both for the fact of revelation and, in the same moment, for the truth of what is revealed. So, for instance, in Mark 2, the paralytic believes both that Jesus is revealing and what he is revealing, namely that Jesus is the

Son of man and that the paralytic's sins are forgiven, because he trusts Jesus' word. But if someone asked him why he was not sinning against the natural light so to do, he will say, "Well, don't you see, I can walk now."

Just as love extends itself into our making promises to God, so faith extends itself to structure our acceptance of his promises to us. We believe he has promised and hope he has, and we hope for the fulfillment of what he promises, on the sole ground that he has promised. But the reasonableness of our hope, should someone ask, and should we have prepared an account as the First Letter of Peter (3:15) admonishes us to do, will be to point to some sign—and, as bearing on hope, this amounts to some surety. So, surety is given by a man who promises so that we may have confidence of fulfillment, of his intention to fulfill. But with God, he gives surety so that we may be confident the promise is spoken at all.

To sum up these last two chapters, we can say that God's promise has a claim to be the pure, perfect form of promising. For it is purely unto the good of those to whom he promises, namely us. It is a good that is him, that is his friendship and so is his truth and is his own good. It is absolutely trustworthy, and as a display, displays the greatest good—God. It is a promise whose trustworthiness can be measured by nothing outside the one who promises. As we might expect, there is a kind of incomparability about the divine promising. By contrast, our promises to God seem in the Old Testament to blend with the obligation we are under to obey his laws and precepts, the obedience that the people promise to live the ordinances of God.

chapter sixteen

::: God's Promises
::: Christologically Determined

I F WE TURN to the New Testament to inform us of the promises of God, all becomes concentrated in the figure of Christ. He gathers to himself all the parts of promising, as it were; he collects in his hands all the reality of promising, both of God's promise to us and our promise—especially under the title of obedience—to God.

First, Christ announces the fulfillment of God's promises. The New Testament begins with the preaching of Jesus, "The time is fulfilled; the kingdom of God is at hand" (Mk 1:15). The fulfillment is a fulfillment of a promise, and harks back to the prophecies of Isaiah:

> How beautiful upon the mountains are the feet of him who brings good tidings [gospel], who publishes peace, who brings good tidings of good, who publishes salvation, who says to Zion, "Your God reigns." (52:7)

In the synagogue at Nazareth, after reading from the scroll of Isaiah, "The Spirit of the Lord is upon me because he has anointed me to preach good news to the poor . . . to proclaim the acceptable year of the Lord," Jesus announces, "Today this scripture has been fulfilled in your hearing" (Lk 4:16–21).

Second, Jesus not only announces fulfillment, but he announces himself as the fulfillment. This, too, is the message of the sermon at the synagogue in Nazareth, for he is the one upon whom the Spirit rests. Again, to the deputation from the imprisoned John the Baptist, Jesus says: "Go and tell John what you see and hear," where what is seen and heard is the fulfillment of Isaiah 29:18 and 35:5–6, that the deaf shall hear, the blind see, and the lame walk, and of 61:1: "the Lord has anointed me to bring good tidings to the afflicted." He is the eschatological herald foretold by Isaiah (52:7), the promised Messiah, as the Father reveals to Peter at Caesarea Philippi (Mk 6; Mt 16), and, at the climax of his trial before the Sanhedrin, the Son of Man whom we will see on the clouds of heaven (Mk 14:62).

In St. Luke's Gospel, Jesus is indicated as himself the fulfillment of God's promises in the three infancy canticles: Mary concludes the Magnificat saying, "He has helped his servant Israel, in remembrance of his mercy, as he spoke [or: as he promised] to our fathers, to Abraham and his posterity, for ever" (1:54–55); Zechariah speaks of God performing "the mercy promised to our fathers," remembering his covenant, keeping oath (1:72, 73); and Simeon, seeing the infant Christ, exclaims, "Lord, now lettest thou thy servant depart in peace, according to thy word [promise]; for mine eyes have seen thy salvation" (2:29–30).[1] And the Gospel fairly ends with the risen Christ explaining to the disciples on the road to Emmaus that his, Jesus', career is the fulfillment of what was promised in Moses and the prophets (24:27).

That Jesus is in this way the fulfillment of God's promise is the presupposition of all the correspondence of St. Paul, who writes that "all the promises of God find their Yes in him" (2 Cor 1:20).

Third, between the public ministry and the trial, there is the Last Supper. "This is my blood of the covenant" (Mk 14:24) or "This cup is the new covenant in my blood" (1 Cor 11:25). Here, he is not only the fulfillment of old promise, but a new promise, the definitive and lasting promise. This cup of shared life recalls the

---

[1] The characterization of Israel as servant as well as talk of rememberance and of mercy is language associated with ancient covenant practice; see Moshe Weinfeld, "Covenant Terminology in the Ancient Near East and its Influence on the West," *Journal of the American Oriental Society* 93 (1973): 190.

communion sacrifices of the old law, and means that the Sinai covenant with its establishment of the Temple sacrifices has been surpassed in being fulfilled.

Because he is Christ, meaning the one anointed with the Holy Spirit, as covenant he is the promised new covenant of Jeremiah. So St. Paul has it, where he styles himself a minister "of a new covenant, not in a written code but in the Spirit," (2 Cor 3:6) "not on tablets of stone but on tablets of human hearts" (3:3). The covenant is written on our hearts, but only because we are in Christ.

Further, already in the Old Testament as we have mentioned, covenant meant communion of life. Here, in the New, Christ is the very communion, the common life shared by us, making us his body. We take the Eucharist so that, living from a *pneumatikos*, spiritual bread, the body of the Christ anointed with *Pneuma*, Spirit, we become one body, one Spirit in him (1 Cor 10).

The communion of life or friendship established by covenant builds on prior friendship, but brings it to a higher pitch. The eternal covenant of Christ means a friendship with God than which no greater can be conceived. Christ's blood and his death are the instrument of this friendship, and their sacrament, the Eucharist, is its sign. "No longer do I call you servants . . . but I have called you friends, for all that I have heard from my Father I have made known to you" (Jn 15:15).

Fourth, there is the Fourth Gospel, which understands Jesus' career as obedient fulfillment of the mission he has received from his Father (especially 5:24, 30, 43; 6:38; 7:16; 8:18; 9:4; 12:49; 14:24). So, on the cross, his "It is finished" declares the discharge of his duty and the performance of his obedience to his Father, whereby he gives us the pattern of ours. Christ is not styled as making promises to his Father, however, for the very reason that St. Thomas gives, namely, that his will needed no steadying by any oath or vow. Just before his passion, when his soul is troubled, he asks: "What shall I say, 'Father, save me from this hour?'" But he answers, "No, for this purpose I have come to this hour" (Jn 12:27). Nonetheless, his obedience remains the standard of ours in the fulfillment of our promises to God. "If you keep my commandments, you will abide in my love, just as I have kept my Father's commandments and abide in his love" (Jn 15:10). Of course, Christ is already upheld as a pattern of obedience by Paul. "Have this mind among yourselves, which is yours in Christ Jesus," in which mind he "became obedient unto death, even death on a cross" (Ph 2:5, 8).

Fifth, Christ is figured by St. Paul not only as fulfillment, but also as one to whom is addressed the promise of God. "The promises were made to Abraham and to his offspring . . . which is Christ" (Gal 3:16). Above, we said God could not promise God; the incarnation makes something possible even for God that otherwise could not be. This is taken up in the next chapter.

Sixth, Christ is also styled as the pledge of God's promise. That is, he is the surety whereby we may be confident God will keep his promise to us. That he is surety and that God gives him as surety is not for the strengthening of his will, or his Father's will, evidently, but for the certainty of our faith and hope. This is a topic of the Letter to the Hebrews.

Seventh and last, Christ, the fulfillment of promise and the promise, makes promises, especially in the last book, the Apocalypse of St. John. "To him who conquers I will grant to eat of the tree of life . . . ; Be faithful unto death, and I will give you the crown of life . . . ; To him who conquers I will give some of the hidden manna, and I will give him a white stone, with a new name written on the stone" (2:7; 2:10; 2:17). The promise of God and the fulfillment of God's promise, Christ, himself makes promises to us, and this is very sweet to the Christian. The promises of Christ, even among divine promises, are altogether singular.

The above seven topics make quite an inventory, wherein Christ is figured variously as announcing fulfillment of past promise, as being the fulfillment of past promise, as the one who receives the promise of God on our behalf, as guarantee or guarantor of the promise God makes to us, and last, as making promises of his own to us.

In the New Testament, therefore, God's promise receives Christological expression, and we could as well say that it is restyled Christocentrically. This does not exclude the pneumatological aspect of this same promise of God, quite the contrary. Christ and the Spirit ought not to be opposed to one another. He who says "Christ," "Anointed," says "anointed with the Spirit" (Acts 2:33; 10:38). So, for the Holy Spirit, we can say in the first place that the Spirit promised by the prophets is now bestowed on Jesus. This we touched upon already above in remembering Luke 4.

From the Anointed One, furthermore, proceeds the Spirit with which all Christians are anointed, as promised by Joel (2:28). So, second, in John's account, the Spirit is explicitly promised by Jesus (Jn 7:37–39). He fulfills this promise when he breathes into the world once again on Easter (20:22) the Spirit he breathed forth from the cross (19:30). For his part, Luke begins the Acts of the Apostles with the notification that the promised Spirit is now bestowed, and he continues to be concerned with this bestowal throughout Acts (e.g., 7:51; 8:14–24; 10:44–47).

Third, the Spirit is also said to be a pledge of God's promise. The God who has destined us for the glory of the resurrection and eternal life "has given us the Spirit as a guarantee" (2 Cor 5:5; cf. 2 Cor 1:22; Eph 1:14). The Spirit through whom God raised Jesus from the dead is the same spirit, now dwelling in us, through whom we shall be raised (Rom 8:11; cf. 1 Cor 15:45).

The Spirit can be styled, thus, as both the substance (second point) and the pledge (third point) of God's promise. He is the pledge in the sense that, keeping the Spirit, and knowing that we do so according as we produce the fruits of the Spirit love—joy, peace, patience, kindness, gentleness, self-control (Gal 5:22–23)—we have assurance that we will be raised up to Christ on the last day, that we shall possess eternal life. But the Spirit can also be figured as the substance of the promise, for it is by the Spirit that we cry out "Abba, Father" (Gal 4:6), and our being taken up into the Trinitarian relations in this way, conformed to the Son so as to be the children of God, is already the boon than which no greater can be conceived.

God's promise to us in Christ is therefore a function of both the mission of the Word and the mission of the Spirit. This is especially apparent in the Letter to the Galatians, and it will be a convenient place to see some of the above relations displayed.   ▪▪

chapter seventeen

Inclusion in Christ:
The Letter to the Galatians

O
UR RECEPTION of the fulfillment of the promise of
God is a receiving of Christ, and it is also a being in
Christ. He is as it were the primary recipient of the promise of God;
he receives it for us, so that we can receive it; and so our reception of
its fulfillment requires us to be in him, to be Christ. We must
become "one person in Christ," as the Eucharistic prayer says. This is
a favorite theme of St. Augustine: "Let us rejoice, then, and give
thanks that we are made not only Christians, but Christ. Do you
understand, brethren, and grasp the grace of God upon us? Marvel,
be glad, we are made Christ. For if he is the head, we are the members: the whole man is He and we."[1] Now, we become one person
with Christ, and get "in" him, by receiving the Holy Spirit. The
Spirit is first Christ's, and conforms us to him, and is the guarantee
that the blessing promised to Abraham, fulfilled in Christ, is also
mediated to us. For his part, St. Augustine often appeals to the Letter to the Galatians in explaining the unity of Christians in the
whole Christ.[2] And, as it happens, Galatians is expressly written to
address a crisis of fidelity, which is to say, a crisis of promise keeping.
"I am astonished that you are so quickly deserting him who called
you in the grace of Christ and turning to a different gospel" (1:6).

---

[1] Tractates on John, XXI, 8 (Nicene and Post-Nicene Fathers, Series I, vol. 7).

[2] See, for example, *Ennaratio in Ps. 100* (3) (CCL 39, 1407–8), and *Ennaratio in Ps. 142* (3) (CCL 40, 2061–62).

The pressure the Galatians are under to abandon the gospel and forsake their promise comes from Judaizers. St. Paul counters this pressure and stiffens the resolve of the Galatians principally by a display of the promise of God, first made to Abraham, now fulfilled in Christ. More importantly and more prominently, however, God's promise in Christ is adduced not just to shore up the Galatians' flagging will but to settle the substantive theological issue raised by the Judaizers. The controversy is a controversy over the nature and fulfillment of God's promise. Is the Law in all its detail, and especially the requirement of circumcision, still in force or not? And this is to ask, Is Christ really the fulfillment of the promise of God, and so as to inaugurate what can rightly be called a new covenant or not? In meeting this issue, there occurs a remarkable moment when Paul styles Jesus not only as the fulfillment of the promise that we receive but also as the one to whom the promise of God is made.

To show the abrogation of the Mosaic covenant with its attendant law, St. Paul reaches back to the covenant made with Abraham. The law of Moses is conceived as an instrument unto the end projected in the covenant with Abraham. Since Christ provides the end to which the first covenant looked forward, the instrument is no longer needed and no longer in play.

More particularly, Paul argues as follows. Those who inherit the promise made to Abraham, Paul says, do so on the basis of faith, not of the works of the law (3:6–9; cf. Rom 4:13). For the law comes 430 years after the promise to Abraham, a promise by God, who does not go back on his word (3:17). The purpose of the law is twofold. First, the law potentiates sin and transforms it into transgression; that is, the law expresses the divine will, and so wrongdoing now appears as contrary to the express will of God (3:19). Second, the law serves as the guardian of an immature recipient of the promise of God. But now both functions have been discharged. As to the first, yes, sin still appears as transgression and "the scripture consigned all things to sin," but this was just in order that "what was promised to faith in Jesus Christ might be given to those who believe" (3:22). Nor is there any longer need of a guardian, for there is now an heir, a Son, Christ himself, who is of age, and we will be of age too if we are in Christ (4:1–4).

As to the promise itself, therefore, the first promise, it is crucial to see that it is not just to Abraham, but to Abraham and to his seed, his offspring. "Now the promises were made to Abraham and to his offspring. It does not say 'And to offsprings,' referring to many; but, referring to one, 'And to your offspring,' which is Christ" (3:16–17). God promises to Christ. The Father makes promises to the Son. But this is in the first place the incarnate Son. What is impossible for the Trinitarian Persons in eternity is possible within the economy of salvation, where the Son is sent in the form of man. Here, there can be promises, requests, prayers, commands, obedience.

This issue repays examination. It was said above that promising depends on the diversity of the wills of the giver and the recipient of the promise. The simplicity of the divine will forecloses the possibility of conceiving the Trinitarian relations in terms of promise, or of command and obedience. But the Son who takes flesh takes also a perfect humanity, which is not perfect except it have within it its own principle of intellectual appetite, or will. So, as the Son sent forth "when the time had fully come" and "born of a woman" (4:4), he has two natures, two wills. There can now be command and obedience and promising because the assumed human will of Christ assures a distinction of wills. Robert Sokolowski:

> It seems that the Incarnation allowed a kind of response by God to God himself to take place, a response that could not have occurred in any other way. . . . The choice of the mission of the Son . . . did not have to happen. It was a determination that need not have occurred. When it did occur as an action, it opened the possibility of a response, of a reaction by another will: the obedient choice of the man Jesus. In becoming obedient to death, even to death on the cross, Jesus allowed an exchange to take place between God's choice and a created counterchoice.
>
> And the eternal Son was the person who made this human choice. It was not just a creature that did so, even though he did

it as a creature. . . . the responses to God's action in the Old Testament were made by people, but in Christ the one who responds
as man is God himself. The splendor of the Redemption lies not
simply in our liberation from sin, but primarily in the admirable
exchange of choices between the creature and God. The Son as
eternal could not have done this.[3]

Just as the Father can command, however, so also he can make
promises to his Son. There can be promises, because the assumed
human will of Christ is a temporally distended will. The Son requires
this kind of will, a human will, so that, like us in all things except sin
(Heb 2:17; 3:15), he can display his identity, which is the identity of
a divine Person, to us who are not eternal. And his Person is displayed to us, across time, in deliberation, choice, expectation, hope,
resolve. And of course it must be that at least one of the two wills
supposed by promising be in time. Once incarnate, he can hear of
what his Father will do before he, the incarnate Son, humanly experiences it. He can imagine what he, the Son, will do before he does
it. He can be recipient of a promise from his Father, and he can
promise his Father. He can be like us in all things but sin.

The Father makes promises to the Son in the first place, therefore, insofar as the Son is incarnate. But in the second place, this is a
matter of our insertion into the Trinitarian economy. That is, the
Father makes promises to the Son precisely insofar as the Son's mission is to redeem us, insofar as the Son is Messiah, insofar as He is
anointed. For if the goods of the promise are first Christ's, the Offspring's, then this fulfillment of the promise to Christ can be good for
us only if we are in Christ. The fulfillment is given to the Head so
that it may be given to us, the members of the body. For us, this
means insertion into the Trinitarian relations. And this happens by
way of the anointing with the Spirit, the same Spirit with which Jesus
is anointed and so *christos*, so that we may be like him in the Spirit as
he is like us in our humanity. This anointing is not separate from our
inclusion in Christ by way of our promising. Our baptism and bap-

---

[3] Robert Sokolowski, *Eucharistic Presence: A Study in the Theology of Disclosure*
(Washington, DC: Catholic University of America Press, 1994), 75.

tismal promising replaces circumcision, and by it we are in Christ and have "put on Christ" (3:27). On the basis of this fundamental conformity to Christ, the Spirit also enables our sanctification by way of a further imitation of Christ and a perfected conformity to Christ, so that, becoming sons after the pattern of Son in the power of the Spirit, we too call out, "Abba, Father" (4:5–6). And this is the pledge of the Spirit, so that we may have good hope for final fulfillment, the resurrection of the flesh and consummation in Christ (cf. Eph 1:14; 2 Cor 5:5). In this way, we can pray with one of the prefaces for Sunday that God "may see and love in us what he sees and loves in Christ."

The content of the promise made to Abraham was, expressly, land and an heir and becoming a great nation. In the context of the letter to the Galatians, it is in the first place the Holy Spirit, and then righteousness, the forgiveness of sins, and adoption as sons. The last three we should understand as a function of the first. All these goods now make up the blessing of Abraham, of which he is the father in faith, because his faith was concretized, but not limited, by the hope of land and heirs, and this the sacrifice of Isaac shows (Heb 11:17ff.). That is, while the promise to Abraham is in terms of land and an heir, his hope in the one who promised and so in the nature of what such a one might mean by making of Abraham a "great nation" survives the test of Genesis 22 and so shows itself to be extended beyond the land and heirs narrowly designated.

Christ first receives what we receive and receives for us. This requires careful expression, however. Does the Offspring fittingly receive all that the offsprings do? If we say that we receive forgiveness, Jesus evidently does not—not for his own sins. Nor can the natural Son receive adoption.[4] But the Spirit he can receive, for this is the anointing that makes him Christ. It is the anointing that, when we receive it, makes us in Christ, makes the whole Christ, Head and members, the anointing by which we are in Christ, and so receive the fulfillment first received, received on our behalf and

---

4 Even within the Trinity, however, he might be said to "receive" his sonship, where this reception is one with being generated.

for us, by the Offspring. As St. Augustine says, "That Spirit by which the Christian is reborn is the same Spirit by which Christ is born. It is the same Spirit that brings about the remission of sins as brought about in Christ that he had no sin."[5]

There is a last question. If the promise addressed to Abraham was received by him, and later by us, in faith, does Christ also receive it by faith? Does he receive the Spirit by faith? If this is to ask whether he receives it by his fidelity to his Father, the answer is Yes. If this is to ask whether he is obedient to his Father's will, the answer is again Yes. "Sacrifices and offerings thou has not desired, but a body hast thou prepared for me; . . . I said, I have come to do thy will, O God." And where the obedience is projected into the future, it takes on the character of the fulfillment of a promise, for, as the quotation the Letter to the Hebrews makes continues, " 'I have come to do thy will, O God,' as it is written of me in the roll of the book" (Heb 10:5, 7, quoting Psalm 39).

But there are other senses of faith that it would not be fitting to impute to him. He knows who he is, the Son of God, and does not believe it as we do. He knows that the Kingdom is at hand, and does not take it on someone's word, as we take it on his. Just as he is the Healer and we the infirm, so we are the ignorant and he the Teacher. He is the pioneer of faith's path, establishing the path we take, and so not believing, but knowing that it is a good path. So, he fittingly receives the promise of God his Father; his agency, in time, is structured by his knowledge of what the Father's will and plan are. On the other hand, while we must believe that God makes promises to us, he knows that his Father makes promises to him.   ▪▪

---

[5] St. Augustine, *On The Predestination of the Saints,* 15(31), in *St. Augustine: Four Anti-Pelagian Writings*, vol. 86 of *The Fathers of the Church*, trans. John A. Mourant (Washington, DC: Catholic University of America Press, 1992), 254.

chapter eighteen

::: Better Hope, Better Surety:
::: The Letter to the Hebrews

A FTER ST. PAUL'S Letter to the Romans, the most extended theological argument of the New Testament is the Letter to the Hebrews. Here, promising appears not incidentally, or in a subterranean way, as might be argued for any important piece of Sacred Scripture, but explicitly, and the concept of promising is central to the argument of the Letter. Especially, the question of the surety for promises given but not yet fulfilled is addressed.

The Letter is occasioned by the impending apostasy of its addressees, perhaps Christians of Jewish provenance living in Rome.[1] Within the Letter, abandoning faith is not distinguished from disobedience (3:10, 12, 16); also, apostasy is equivalent to abandoning hope (6:6, 11); especially important for us, apostasy and infidelity are expressed in terms of forsaking the promise of God and disregarding the oath he swears to us (4:1; 6:13). And how does the Letter try to head off apostasy? Principally, the Letter's strategy is nothing except to manifest the effectiveness, the finality, the certainty—the sheer splendor—of the promise of God in Christ.

The promise of God in Christ constitutes a better covenant than the Sinai covenant. In the language of the Letter, it is a perfect covenant; that is, it makes the Sinai covenant what it wants to be. This new and perfect covenant is established by a new and perfect

---

[1] F. F. Bruce, *The Epistle to the Hebrews,* rev. ed. (Grand Rapids, MI: Eerdmans, 1990), 14.

sacrifice; and this new sacrifice requires a new priesthood. The better covenant, better sacrifice, better priesthood should elicit in us a better hope, a perfect hope whose anchor will be in the sanctuary where the better priest has entered (6:19–20).

In fact, the Letter proceeds in the reverse order. It moves from the better priest (7:1–10) to a new law and regulation of the priesthood (7:11–28) to a better ministry (8:1–6) to a better covenant (8:7–13), thence to new rites (chapter 9) and last to a better sacrifice (chapter 10). Briefly: (1) the priesthood is better because it is "according to the order of Melchizedek," to whom Abraham paid tithes, and so not according to mere human generation from Abraham; (2) the conditions of priesthood change, in that it is now exercised by one man and one time for all; (3) the priestly ministry is better, for it is exercised in the true tent, the heavenly temple; (4) the covenant is better, for it is written in hearts; (5) the rites themselves are better, since effected not with the blood of goats or calves but in Christ's own blood; and (6) the sacrifice is better, for unlike the old sacrifices, it is effective for the cleansing of consciences.

In fact, all is contained in the "better priest," and subsequent reflection is a function of Christological meditation. We are interested especially in seeing how Christ functions also as surety for the new covenant his priesthood brings with it. The Letter begins to close on this topic by reaching back behind the Sinai covenant, as did St. Paul in Galatians, to the covenant with Abraham.

As was the promise to Abraham, so the new covenant is established by an oath. Where the oath to Abraham was by "his name," since God has no one greater than himself to swear by (6:13), the oath establishing the new priesthood, and so the new covenant, is by Jesus:

> Those who formerly became priests took their office without an oath, but this one was addressed with an oath, "The Lord has sworn and will not change his mind, "Thou art a priest forever." This makes Jesus the surety of a better covenant. (7:21–22)

The oath is addressed to Jesus, and it is promised to him that he be a priest, but it makes of Jesus a surety for us, a surety for the new and better covenant. "Surety" *(egguos)* might also be "guarantor." It is the difference between saying "I swear by this deposit (which I forfeit if I do not fulfill the promise)" and "I swear by George (who undertakes to see that the promise is fulfilled)." It makes no difference in reading the text, however, for in either case, Jesus supplies for the new covenant what the name of God did for the promise to Abraham.

The possibility of such a parallel to the promise to Abraham rests on the divinity of Jesus, the fact that he is the co-equal Son of God. For as the Letter says at 6:13, there is nothing superior to God by which he swears, by which he can give surety to us. Because he is the Son, and "bears the very stamp of his [God's] nature" (1:3), Jesus has the wherewithal to function as "the name" of God; he can be the very presence of God, and his engagement of himself will be God his Father's engagement of himself.

When we trust God on the basis of this surety, therefore, we by no means measure his promise by something outside himself and subject him to what is beneath him. If Jesus were not divine, it would be so, and we should be subjecting the promise and covenant of God to an outside and necessarily blasphemous test. And did we not confess the divinity of Jesus, we should by that fact fail to make covenant with the true God; holding the Son up to contempt (cf. 6:6), we would denigrate the covenant of which he is the surety.

The engagement of the Son as the surety God gives is displayed across his sacrificial death. To see this, we need merely continue the argument of the Letter in chapter 7. Jesus is the surety of the new covenant in that he is the priest established by this covenant. And it is a better covenant because its priesthood is superior.[2] First, the superiority consists in the fact that this priesthood is established by an oath, as we have seen. Second, as it is subsequently explained, it is superior because "he holds his priesthood permanently" and "is always living to make intercession" (7:24, 25). Third, the priesthood is superior because this priest is "holy, blameless, unstained," and "has no need, like those [former] high priests, to offer sacrifices daily, first for his own sins and then for those of the people" (7:26, 27).

---

[2] Bruce, *Hebrews,* 170–79.

The first and the third reasons for the superiority of his priest-hood lead to his divinity. The second reason, however, leads to the question of surety. He holds his priesthood permanently and is always living to intercede for us because he enters into the eternal, heavenly sanctuary. As was said earlier in the Letter, he has "become a priest . . . by the power of an indestructible life" (7:16). This seems to say, in other words, that he becomes a priest by his very entrance into the sanctuary, where he makes sacrifice. Now, as is explained later, this sanctuary is the heavenly and eternal sanctuary (9:11ff.). He enters this sanctuary by his death. So, summing up, we are given to say that he becomes a priest by his death on the cross. For the same reason, that he becomes a priest by passing into heaven, the sacrifice is also to be described as taken into the eternal sanctuary, and therefore, he offers sacrifice but once, and not day after day.

We are now at the climax and term of the development from better priest, to better covenant, to better sacrifice. The sacrifice is better because of the excellence of the victim, who enters the sanc-tuary not with the blood of bulls and calves, but with his own blood (9:12). But also, the sacrifice is better because of where it is offered; also, it is better because it is more efficacious for the cleansing of consciences (10:1ff.). It is a sacrifice for a covenant wherein covenant betrayals can be mended. This is altogether crucial to apprehending the finality of the new covenant. It is final because the sacrifice of Jesus can expiate the sin even of those who refuse the covenant or violate it.[3]

All is concentrated in the death of the Christ. Ordinarily, death exempts the one who promises, or his guarantor, from further duty; here, the death of the Lord is the fulfillment of his role as security for and guarantor of the better covenant. It is through his death that he becomes priest and accedes to heaven, the heavenly sanctuary where he is always living to make intercession.

The sacrifice in his blood, his death, is accomplished on Calvary and established eternally in heaven in the power of an indestructible

---

[3] See Ben F. Meyer, *The Aims of Jesus* (London: SCM Press, 1979), 216–19.

life, which is to say, by the resurrection. At the same time, and notwithstanding that he lives, for the very reason that the sacrifice that establishes the new covenant is of course a death, the death of the mediator, the covenant it establishes is also a testament, in the sense of a "last will and testament" (9:15–17). This is the mechanism of our entrance into covenant blessings, the expression in legal categories of how the death of the Lord benefits us. The covenant with us is effected by the better sacrifice of the better priest, which is his death, which makes of the covenant a testament.[4] The death of the Lord is the condition of our entry into the new covenant, therefore, in two senses seemingly at odds with one another. First, the death enables us to inherit covenant blessing as from the deceased, but also, second, this covenant depends on Christ's being an eternal priest in the eternal sanctuary, with a blood that "speaks more graciously than the blood of Abel" (12:24)—more graciously, since it leads to the cleansing of consciences, not the branding of Cain.

The surety, therefore, in the end, is the death of the Lord, which the resurrection makes manifest in its character as the death of the Son. As in the Old Testament, where the pledge was God's word, name, self, so in the New Testament is it his Son as dying for us. Thus, it is the pledge of Trinitarian love: the Father loves us at the price of his Son, as his Son, as sons. This is the answer to the question of what surety we might have for the promise of God, the promise finally delivered and articulated in so startling a way through Jesus (chapter 16). As he enters into the heavenly sanctuary, so also does our hope, and he becomes surety, "a sure and steadfast anchor of the soul, a hope that enters into the inner shrine behind the curtain, where Jesus has gone as a forerunner on our behalf" (3:18–19).

That he is in this way, through his death and only so, the surety of our hope, the letter says quite clearly:

---

4 Myles M. Bourke, "The Epistle to the Hebrews," in *The Jerome Biblical Commentary* (Englewood Cliffs, NJ: Prentice-Hall, 1968), 61: 54: "What verifies the testament concept in the case of the new covenant is that it did involve the death of the one who initiated it; hence he is not only one who established the covenant, but also the testator."

> As it is, we do not yet see everything in subjection to him. But we see Jesus, who for a little while was made lower than the angels, crowned with glory and honor because of the suffering of death, so that by the grace of God he might taste death for every one. (2:8–9)

Because we *see*, because the resurrection is given us in some way, and itself gives us the one who tasted death for all, our obedience and faith are made strong. The crucified and resurrected Jesus is given to us as a sign, the great sign, as is clear from the context of the passage just quoted.

> How shall we escape if we neglect such a great salvation? It was declared at first by the Lord, and it was attested to us by those who heard him, while God also bore witness by signs and wonders and various miracles and by gifts of the Holy Spirit. (2:3–4)

That he himself did not seek surety enters into his being a surety for us. This is shown first by his obedience: "although he was a Son, he learned obedience through what he suffered" (5:8). True obedience requires a kind of not-knowing, wherein one has simple trust in the one who commands. Now, Jesus knows what he is doing and what he is accomplishing. But his human knowledge does not extend to that comprehensive vision according to which he sees that the command he executes is the best ordering of things possible. For that, he trusts his Father.[5]

Second, Jesus is the pioneer and forerunner of our faith (12:2). Now it is the part of the pioneer not to find the blazes and hash marks that indicate he is on the right path, but to put them there for others to see so that they can be confident they are on the right path. If he knows where he is going, still, no one else has been there before. Not even God his Father has been there *before*, for the very good reason that eternity is not the experience of before and after, of anticipation and fulfillment. This means that he must exercise his faithfulness to God without his Father's presence and so *a fortiori* without proof of this presence. The cry of dereliction, therefore—"My God, my

---

[5] Bernard Lonergan, *De Verbo Incarnato* (Rome: Gregorian University Press, 1961), 421–24.

God, why hast thou forsaken me?" (Mk 15:34)—is not foreign to Hebrews: "In the days of his flesh, Jesus offered up prayers and supplications, with loud cries and tears, to him who was able to save him from death, and he was heard for his godly fear" (5:7).

Therefore are we to imitate "the pioneer and perfecter of our faith" (12:2) by not breaking faith; rather should we follow the example of him to whose obedience and fidelity a great cloud of witness bears testimony in chapter 11. If we have really been "looking to Jesus" (12:2) in this way, then we will lift our drooping hands and strengthen our weak knees (12:12).

As with ordinary promises, this promise of God in Christ is a device to conquer time. It is not, doubtless, that the eternal God needs to conquer it for himself. But for our part, we need to have his eternity conquer our time. Just so, this conquering of time is not by an anticipation of future action on the basis of the memory of the promise, but by eternity itself. An ordinary promise unites past, present, and future; but God's promise depends on the one moment of eternity to which all our times are present. This is why our hope in God's promise is so certain. It is a promise than which no greater can be made, where eternity is pledged for time's sake, the time of the life of our being saved. And this first reason for our certainty is completed by a second. This has to do with the nature of God's eternity. For it is the eternity, not of a divinity "en bloc," or of the divine unity as such, or of a knowing and loving without any internal articulation. It is rather the eternity of the Trinitarian relations. It is into these relations that we are taken up by the one who was not ashamed to call us brethren (2:11). This is to say it is an eternity of love that is the guarantee for time and that goes bail for it. ∷

chapter nineteen

Our Promise to God as a Personal Mission from God

W E TURN NOW to our promises to God, for whose keeping the Letter to the Hebrews says, we should lift our drooping hands and strengthen our weak knees (12:12). How do we do this, if the argument of chapter 7 is not mistaken, except by keeping our eye on the Christian good, the properly Christian content, of what we promise?

Of course, there is the example of the Lord's obedience, and there is the surety he offers for God's promise, giving us heart to stay faithful ourselves. As to example, strictly, as we have said reporting St. Thomas, the Lord is beyond promising anything to his Father. He may promise us. And his Father may promise him. But we do not read that he promises his Father. Promising requires that there be two wills, and that one of them be in time, as we have noted. But also, there must be some point to the promising. God cannot be helped in his providence by any temporal promise, even that of his Son, and the Son cannot by promising shore up his human will, already immovably fixed on the good he is to do. On the other hand, there is the good of display, of expressing a love complete in the comprehensiveness of its dedication and the fixity of its resolve. It is this that Hans Urs von Balthasar gets at when he speaks as if the Lord does promise, does make a vow, to his Father.[1] Balthasar points out that vows bespeak two things. They can be a

---

1 Hans Urs von Balthasar, *The Christian State of Life*, trans. Sister Mary Frances McCarthy (San Francisco: Ignatius Press, 1983), 198.

means unto greater love, as well as an expression of great love already exercised.[2] As means, vows befit those on the way to perfect love, whose will needs shoring up; as expressions, their model is in Christ and our Lady.

There is thus a kind of supereminence in the relation of the Son, the incarnate Son, to the Father, and his obedience is the model of ours. But also, beyond example, there is Christ himself, in his reality, the very reality of him that we participate in by grace, through the pledge of the Spirit that has been given us. What I mean to say is that, beyond the promising and obedience we render as imitations of Christ's act of obedience, there is also the content of our promise as something in Christ, as a participation in him. Our being in Christ is by way of a promise; also, *what* we promise is in him. This is so because what we promise is our mission, and every Christian mission is a share in the mission of Christ. Corresponding to his obedience is our promised obedience. But as his obedience is in fulfillment of a mission, so our promise is to a share in his mission. If we take up this great theme of Hans Urs von Balthasar and turn it to our purposes, we shall say that in order to keep our promises, our admiration of, and wonder at, and love of the Lord in his humility and obedience unto death, in fulfillment of his Father's will, in discharge of his mission, must be adjusted so that, contemplating his mission, we contemplate our own, as well.[3] When we do so, we shall be contemplating nothing less than that gift of God to us that makes us what he wishes us to be eternally in his sight.[4]

Mission is especially the topic of the Fourth Gospel. The very Person of the incarnate Lord is, in St. John's presentation, nothing except his hearing of the Father, his obedience to the command of the Father, his fulfillment of the mission he has received from the Father. But—and this is the important thing for our promises—this

---

[2] Ibid., 64, 162

[3] Ibid., 72–83; see also Hans Urs von Balthasar, *Theo-Drama: Theological Dramatic Theory*, vol. 3: *Dramatis Personae: Persons in Christ*, trans. Graham Harrison (San Francisco, CA: Ignatius, 1992), 230–59, 263–82.

[4] For the religious life as gift, for instance, see John Paul II, *Vita Consecrata*, 20.

mission is extended to us. "As the Father has sent me, so I send you" (Jn 20:21; cf. 17:18). And most explicitly, in the High Priestly Prayer of chapter 17: "For I have given them the words which thou gavest me, and they have received them and know in truth that I came from thee" (17:8); and "They are not of the world, even as I am not of the world" (17:16); and "As thou didst send me into the world, so I have sent them into the world" (17:18); and "Father, I desire that they also, whom thou hast given me, may be with me where I am, to behold my glory which thou hast given me before the foundation of the world" (17:23).

Now, the good we promise God as Christians is nothing but the mission we receive from him, and it is a participation in the mission of Christ, who is himself the new promise, himself the pledge that God is faithful and cannot deny himself (2 Tim 2:13).

The Lord's mission, as Balthasar says, just is his Person; it is his Person as displayed in the world, in the economy of salvation.[5] His human history shows who he is, and the achievement of his mission is in part the achievement of this display. Our mission, received as a participation in him, is something we must achieve, too; but by contrast, our history will construct, and not just show, who we are.

Charles Taylor takes personal identity to mean centrally the ensemble of fundamental evaluations and appreciations, choices and decisions, that frame how the world appears to us and dictates our actions:

> My identity is defined by the commitments and identifications which provide the frame or horizon within which I can try to determine from case to case what is good, or valuable, or what ought to be done, or what I endorse or oppose. In other words, it is the horizon within which I am capable of taking a stand.[6]

If this is what constitutes the core of personal identity, then finding our mission in Christ is finding who we are, or who we are supposed

---

5 Balthasar, *Theo-Drama,* vol. 3, 149–59.
6 Charles Taylor, *Sources of the Self: The Making of the Modern Identity* (Cambridge, MA.: Harvard University Press, 1989), 27.

to be. Actually becoming who we are supposed to be will be the enactment of the mission, the realization and embodiment of the evaluations and decisions that are the soul of the tasks comprising the mission. The narrative of this becoming, including the events in which I am targeted by the actions of others and treated in the way I am because of my mission, will comprise, if perfect, the complete description of my personal identity.[7] Of course, we expect this perfect tale to be told only in the Book of Life, by the one who is worthy to open the scroll of history, and that is why the true name of our identity must an eschatological gift (Rev 2:17). This is the answer, the Christian answer, to the question of destiny raised in chapter 9.

It can seem that we rejoin Nietzsche at this point: to be forsworn is to lose one's self; to break one's promise is to cease to have a self. Only those who promise—and only those who promise Christianly—have a self, a self that will last and be saved up for the last day, and that can receive an abiding name. "For whoever would save his life will lose it; and whoever loses his life for my sake and the gospel's will save it" (Mk 8:35). But the differences from Nietzsche cannot go unmentioned. The Christian self is a received self, and we receive our personal identities, our missions, from God. Nietzsche's self is wholly self-made, and that is supposed to be part of the glory of the new man. The post-Christian man is therefore to make something, himself, from nothing, and with what success we see more easily every day. There is also a contrast to be drawn between the destiny of an eternal identity and the destiny of an eternal return.

To conclude this chapter, in light of the Johannine emphasis on Christ's obedience, we can say that, though he makes no promise, Christ is the pattern of, gives power for, and represents us in our obedience and so in our discharge of our promise to God. In this way, he is our promise to God. But then, if we put this moment from the Fourth Gospel together with the Last Supper, we will say he is both our promise to God and God's promise to us. For at the

---

[7] For narrativity and personal identity, see Taylor, 47ff. For personal identity as constituted also by the actions of others of which I am a target, see Robert Sokolowski, *Moral Action* (Bloomington, IN: Indiana University Press, 1985), 61.

Supper, his blood, he himself, is the new and everlasting Covenant. Taking both ways together is to say that he is the mediator, not as some neutral standing between two parties, but as engaging himself to both, for both, representing each to the other.

chapter twenty
Baptismal Promises

O UR PARTICIPATION in the mission of Christ is sacramentally enacted and effected in baptism. There can be subsequent determinations of our mission in marriage, orders, and religious life, but baptism is basic. It is the universal sacrament of Christian mission, of sharing in the mission of Christ.

We speak of baptismal promises. What exactly are they? In the Roman Rite, there is no explicit promise with the very words "I promise" made to God or to the Church to do anything. What there is instead is a profession of faith according to the ancient threefold interrogation, bearing on the Persons of the Trinity. Just before the profession, however, there is a *rejection* of promises, in the renunciation of Satan "and all his empty promises."

"Empty promises" translates the Latin *pompae*, or "pomps" as we used to say in an older translation.[1] Originally, moreover, there was only one pomp *(pompa)* to renounce, according to Hippolytus of Rome, reporting the early-third-century Roman liturgy. The one to be baptized renounced Satan, his pomp, and his works. Now, a *pompa* could be a solemn procession, a train or retinue, a parade or display. For Tertullian, it probably meant the spectacle of a circus procession, which usually included within it a procession of idols and images.[2]

---

1 For what follows, see M.-E. Boismard, OP, " 'Je renonce à Satan, à ses pompes et à ses oeuvres . . . ,'" *Lumière et Vie* 26 (March 1956): 105–10.

2 J. H. Waszink, "Pompa Diaboli," *Vigiliae Christianae* 1 (1947): 33–34.

Pompa comes over from the Greek *pompê*, a sending or dispatching, and also, a solemn procession. *Pompê* in turn is likely a translation of the Hebrew *mela'kah*, the original sense of which would have been "works," where Satan's works are sins.[3] One is released from Satan and his works as were the Israelites released from Pharaoh and his "works"—the labor undertaken at his order—so as to turn to the worship of God in the wilderness (Ex 5:3–4). So, before baptism, whose type is release from the servitude of Pharaoh in crossing the Red Sea, one renounces Satan and his works, that is, sinning, which constitutes the cult or worship of Satan.

"Works" is thus the closest rendering of the sense of the original rite. The translations of the Hebrew by "angels" or *"pompê"* were mistakes understandable because angels and sendings and works all have the same root in Hebrew. It is the full breadth of the Greek *pompê*, sending, that then gives us the sense of cortege, display, and spectacle. Circus processions were especially spectacular, and associated with idols. Even so, idolatry and vanity, as works of Satan, can easily stand for all sins, and so the (mis)translation turns out to work very nicely.

What about our own "empty promises"? This works well, too. From the sense of display we can easily slip to "mere or false display," and so "vanity," as showing something in a light other than it is, and as it were promising a thing's being and power falsely. The seductions of Satan to sin are all of them indeed false promises. Eat this and your eyes will be opened, and you will be like God, knowing good and evil. True, as to a sort of knowing of good and evil; false as to knowing them in the way of a practical knowledge determining what good and evil are; both true and false as to opened eyes; absolutely false as to being like God.

A perfect contrast with the renunciation of Satan's promises would consist in an acceptance of God's promises. This is rather presupposed. The question remains, what are the promises the one who is baptized makes to God? In the first place, there is a promise to believe, as indicated by the profession of faith that follows the

---

[3] Boismard, "'Je renounce,'" 108–9.

renunciation of Satan. This is manifested again further in the rite by the word of address that accompanies the lighted candle the neophyte receives, wherein he is exhorted to keep the light of faith alive until kingdom come. Also, the white garment in which the neophyte is clothed is to be brought unstained by the works of sin to the judgment of God on the last day.

Other material scattered through the Rite of Christian Initiation for Adults mentions or supposes the idea of promising. "When they are baptized, they should not receive such a sacrament passively, for of their own will they enter into a covenant with Christ, rejecting their errors and adhering to the true God" (30). In the second stage of initiation, immediately preparatory to baptism at the end of Lent, the candidates are enrolled, writing their names in the book "as a pledge of fidelity" (22). Before this enrollment, candidates are to give evidence not only of a "sufficient knowledge of Christian teaching" and of "a sense of faith and charity," but of "conversion of mind and morals" (23). One of the prayers for the chosen candidates expressly mentions the new covenant these "children of the promise" enter into (149).

In fact, the idea of a baptismal promising, of a baptismal covenant with God, is very prominent in the fathers. Cyril of Jerusalem and Ambrose report that the candidates face the west to renounce Satan and his pomp and works, and then turn to the east to make the profession of faith. The contrast of renunciation and commitment is thus inscribed in bodily gesture.[4] Cyril, John Chrysostom, and Theodore of Mopsuestia interpret the renunciation as breaking a contract with Satan, and the profession of faith as

---

4 Hugh M. Riley, *Christian Initiation: A Comparative Study of the Interpretation of the Baptismal Liturgy in the Mystagogical Writings of Cyril of Jerusalem, John Chrysostom, Theodore of Mopsuestia, and Ambrose of Milan*, vol. 17 of *Studies in Christian Antiquity*, ed. Johannes Quasten (Washington, DC: Catholic University of America Press, 1974), 24–28. Riley raises the question of Cyril's authorship of the Mystagogical Lectures on 11. For a more recent discussion of authorship, see Auguste Piédagnel, in Cyrille de Jérusalem, *Catéchèses Mystagogiques, Sources Chrétiennes*, vol. 126bis (Paris: Editions du Cerf, 1988), 177–87. Although he judges the text certainly later than 380, Piédagnel holds to Cyril's primary authorship, with the final redaction by John of Jerusalem.

entering into a contract with Christ. Cyril tells the neophytes, "When you renounce Satan, trampling under foot all covenant with him, you break the ancient treaties with hell."[5] John Chrysostom likens the contract with Christ to a nuptial bond, where the profession of faith is as a dowry given to the Bridegroom.[6] "Just as there was a previous contract with Satan, so too, the verbal act established a new, solemn contract with Christ. Indeed, the candidate utters the formula, but once uttered it has binding, transcendental consequences." All four fathers have "recourse to specific legal terminology in describing the act as a binding contract."[7]

But still, what then is the content of the promise with God? How is it specified? Fundamentally, it is specified in the rite itself, more apparent in the ancient form of triple immersion. From the fourth century lecture to the newly baptized at Jerusalem:

> you were conducted to the sacred pool of divine Baptism, as Christ passed from the cross to the sepulchre you see before you. You were asked, one by one whether you believed in the name of the Father and of the Son and of the Holy Spirit; you made that saving confession, and then you dipped thrice under water and thrice rose up again, therein mystically signifying Christ's three days burial. . . . Baptism not only washes away our sins and procures for us the gift of the Holy Spirit, but it is also the antitype [or representation, sacrament, counterpart] of the Passion of Christ.[8]

The lecturer is as it were expanding on Romans 6: baptism is baptism into the death of Christ, and the elements of the rite bespeak the discrete events of the passion in similar detail. Evidently, therefore, what one takes on in baptism is Christ, a share in Christ, a share in his very mission as culminating in the cross, and this is signified as much by the action as by the words of the ritual. So to live

---

[5] Riley, *Christian Initiation*, 92.

[6] Ibid., 100.

[7] Ibid., 102–3.

[8] Mystagogical Lecture II, 2–6, in *The Works of Saint Cyril of Jerusalem*, vol. 2, trans. Leo P. McCauley and Anthony A. Stephenson, *The Fathers of the Church*, vol. 64 (Washington, DC: Catholic University of America Press, 1970), 163–66. Stephenson thinks Cyril is unlikely to have written these lectures.

is the good one promises. A share in the mission of Christ, as crowned by his resurrection, is the good eliciting the love of the baptized, such that the love of self becomes submerged in the love of Christ, and one does not want to love oneself or one's good except they be in Christ.

There is a good reason why the content of the promise does not come to fuller expression in words. The very completeness of what one engages and its transcendent and divine character require that it be signified more as a being taken over by Christ than as a discrete thing "promised" by an agent who remains what he is throughout the event. In this promise, one's agency is engaged so as to have one's agency transformed. One becomes a "new creation" in Christ, and there is something odd about styling what is created as an agent of that creation. To make one's baptismal promises, so to speak, is more to let oneself be remade than to celebrate one's own agency. This is what the rite conveys.

To renounce Satan and his empty promises suggests a contrast, as noted, to God and his promises. If Satan's promises are empty, God's must be full. If a promise is empty because the one who makes it does not intend to keep it and has not the power to keep it, then by contrast, trusting ourselves to God means trusting one who both intends to keep and can keep his promises. We are targeting God's veracity and his power. And, given the sorts of things he promises, we are targeting his veracity as trustworthy in itself, since it cannot be shown to be trustworthy by something outside it. And we trust God's power, his omnipotence, which we must think to be engaged in such things as the incarnation of the Son of God, and the resurrection of the flesh, Christ's and ours, all of which things form the content of the profession of faith.

Renouncing Satan and turning to God is a matter of promising to renounce the one whose promises are empty; it is promising to trust the one whose promising is a promising than which no greater can be conceived.

chapter twenty-one

Religious and Priestly
and Married Promises

D EVOTION IS a religious act. It is the consecration of
oneself, as it were, a vowing of oneself *(de-vovere)* to
God. St. Thomas counts devotion as the first of the interior acts of
religion, and notes that of itself, devotion produces joy, since it
unites us to God, the infinite good.[1] Devotion finds expression,
moreover, in vowing, one of the exterior acts of religion.[2] This is to
say that, usually, a Christian's mission, his share in the mission of
Christ, involves promising of some sort beyond the promises of
baptism. Ordinarily, on the basis of baptism, there are further
promises, and these promises too are religiously characterized. Most
Christians marry, and their marriage vows are religiously determined promises. Some Christians make promises of stability in a
monastery and conversion of life, or of poverty, chastity, and obedience, by which they become "religious" in the sense of becoming a
nun or monk or friar.[3] In the west, priests promise celibacy, and
that assimilates them to religious, although, obviously, there is
something specific about promising to be a priest just as such.

---

[1] *Summa theologiae* II–II, Q. 82, aa. 1 and 4.

[2] *Summa theologiae* II–II, Q. 88.

[3] The structure of promising for those who belong to so-called secular institutes
recognized by the Roman Church is somewhat different: perpetual incorpora-
tion into the institute means that temporary promises are always to be renewed.
See *Codex Iuris Canonici*, c. 723.

These promises, if lived out thoroughly and conscientiously, govern and give shape to the entire subsequent ensemble of the person's experiences, understandings, and choices, especially as these relate us to other persons, and especially insofar as understanding and choice are consolidated in fundamental outlook and habitual response. This shaped ensemble of conscious acts and habits is the "person" one becomes in Christ, one's "personal identity" in the modern sense. According as the assembling of this shaped ensemble is patient to the continued promptings of grace, it just is one's continuous share in the mission of Christ.

In this chapter, we first note some differences between kinds of post-baptismal promises, and then second, an important similarity. Third, there is a special question about whether it is proper to speak of marriage as a vocation. Fourth, the question of the obliging character of the goods embraced in these promises is addressed, and last, their common foundation in Christ is noted.

The structure of such post-baptismal promises is not all the same. Married people promise one another, before God, the Church witnessing.[4] Although marrying was probably always a religious act, still, today anyway, one can think of people marrying one another and exchanging promises, but not before God, and calling no religious community to witness. Marriage, though it seems to be less successful in a secular age, still can make sense, and so marriage promises can still be undertaken apart from Christianity.

Religious vows, on the other hand, are not made before God, but to God, with the Church again as witness. They do not have a context that would make them intelligible apart from the Church. They do not have a purely natural context, and, apart from the Fall

---

[4] To be sure, in Christian sacramental marriage one has also a duty to God—so, for instance, to keep's one's faith with him by bringing up to the worship of God the children that are made in the image of God (*Summa theologiae* Suppl. Q. 65, a. 2, ad 5). Even so, the object of the marriage consent is the power to have sexual relations (Q. 48, a. 1, c). It is this power that spouse surrenders to spouse (Q. 53, a. 2, c), and thus the promises that constitute marriage as marriage are exchanged by the spouses, made by the spouses to one another. A religious commends his body to God and contracts with God; married people contract with one another (Q. 61, a. 1, c and ad 3; and Q. 53, a. 1, ad 1).

and the Christian understanding of the Fall and sin and subsequent redemption, they would not take place. They are promises that call more directly upon our faith in the revealed promises of God to us. And in this way, religious seem to enter more emphatically or obviously into the "pledge" character of Christ himself, such as is displayed in the Letter to the Hebrews. That is, religious take on themselves some of the character of being a surety for the promises of God. This is often gotten at by speaking of the value of religious life as an "eschatological witness." Religious life makes no sense unless the promises of God are true and real, and there is saved up for all Christians a crown of glory.

Priestly promises have especially to do with Christ and the Church. Of all the states of Christian life, priesthood is most obviously a share in the mission of Christ, for the priest undertakes to represent Christ as himself sent as Head and Spouse to his body, the Church, and in his offices of teaching, ruling, and sanctifying.[5] "He called to him those whom he desired . . . and he appointed twelve to be with him, and to be sent out to preach and have authority to cast out demons" (Mk 3:13–14). The priest is first to be with Christ and then to be sent out. He is sent from Christ and to the Church, and he is therefore engaged to both, though to the Church on the basis of his engagement to Christ.[6]

What is the same in marriage vows, priestly celibacy, and religious chastity, it will be noted, is that they all bear on the body and the sexuality of the body. Life promises, which look toward death, are dispositions of the procreative power that looks beyond it.[7] We touch here on what Pope John Paul II calls the "nuptiality" of the body.[8] It is in and through the body that persons can make that complete donation of themselves in freedom they are called to, and

---

[5] See the Second Vatican Council, *Lumen gentium*, 18, and *Presbyterorum ordinis*, 2.

[6] John Paul II, *Pastores Dabo Vobis*, 15–16.

[7] See Ghislain Lafont, *Imagining the Catholic Church: Structured Communion in the Spirit* (Collegeville, MN: Liturgical Press, 2000), 111–13, 114–15.

[8] John Paul II, *The Theology of the Body: Human Love in the Divine Plan* (Boston, MA: Pauline Books and Media, 1997), 60–63.

this is true in both married life and religious life. The freedom of self-gift is not realized except across and in the body. Moreover, the concern with the body in these life promises has also to do with the temporal dimension of promising. By our bodies, we are in that realm of half actuality, where there can be such a thing as progress, a further realization of act in potency, a further shaping of what can have but does not yet have the shape of maturity. By our bodies, in other words, we are in time, and so are liable to engage in promising. Our temporality brings with it one of the conditions of promising.

Promising is not an affair of freedom alone, but an affair of timed, embodied freedom, and it is appropriate that the content of life-promising concern the body. It must be that for human beings really to dispose themselves wholly and in freedom toward some other person, a central concern is the body. Promising it, we take charge of one of the conditions of promising. By taking care that the decision of freedom is a decision that bears precisely on the body, we make freedom, human freedom, real.

There can seem to be a problem with including marriage promises as a determination of a Christian's mission. Because marriage is an "office of nature" before being a sacrament of the Church, because it is the usual state of Christian life, and because its promises are directed immediately to the spouses, it has not always been customary to speak of married life as a "mission," or to speak of a "call" to marriage and family life. It was assumed that a call was only to priestly or religious life. Hans Urs von Balthasar takes that view:

> No sound and balanced Christian will ever say of himself that he chose marriage by virtue of a divine election, an election comparable to the election and vocation experienced or even perceived by those called to the priesthood or to the personal following of Christ in religious life.[9]

Yves Congar, on the other hand, proposes rather to distinguish vocations based in the order of creation and vocations based in the

---

[9] Hans Urs von Balthasar, *The Christian State of Life*, trans. Sister Mary Frances McCarthy (San Francisco: Ignatius Press, 1983), 421.

order of grace. Both are true vocations, though the latter are more urgent and more strictly so-called.[10] Even so, the Incarnation gives created realities, including marriage, "a divine significance, which belongs to the wisdom of faith."[11]

For its part, the Second Vatican Council speaks in *Lumen gentium* (31) of a special vocation of the laity "to seek the kingdom of God by engaging in temporal affairs and directing them according to God's will," and in the Decree on the Apostolate of the Laity (11) of the "apostolate of married persons and of families." In his 1994 "Letter to Families," John Paul II says that the apostles "came to understand that marriage and family are a true vocation which comes from God himself and is an apostolate: the apostolate of the laity."[12] The Apostolic Exhortation *Familiaris Consortio* frequently speaks of the "mission" of married people, of parents, of the family.[13] The importance of the issue may be put as follows. Balthasar wants a young man to ask himself, "Am I called to the priesthood or not?" The Holy Father lets him ask, "Am I called to the priesthood or to married life?"

Granted the providence of God, which is complete, and granted the taking up of marriage into the supernatural order, so that it directly bears on things touching our final end, it seems impossible to resist the view of the Council and of the Holy Father.[14] We can therefore relate all Christian promises, including those of marriage, to the Christian's share in the mission of Christ. In this way, we make more apparent the great goods Christian promising engages.

We should ask again in the context of Christian promising about the obliging character of these goods. If it is the good that obliges, as is the argument of this book, do the great goods of marriage and the priesthood and religious life oblige before they are vowed? As the obligation to tell the truth is there, already, before I

---

[10] Yves Congar, OP, *Lay People in the Church*, rev. ed., trans. Donald Attwater (Westminster, MD: Newman Press, 1965), 427–32.

[11] Ibid., 431.

[12] See no. 18. The same thing seems implicit in the Apostolic Exhortation of 1988, *Christifideles Laici*, if 56, 57, and 58 are taken together.

[13] For instance, at 6, 17, 38, 39 47, 49, 50–54, 57, 62, 66, 69, 71.

[14] Lafont, *Imagining the Catholic Church*, 113–14, speaks indifferently of vocation to both religious and married life.

swear on the Bible, is the obligation to do these things there, before
I promise? The trouble with saying Yes is that we seem to land in
the absurdity of being obliged to do incompatible things. This is
where comes in the importance of realizing that what we promise
Christianly is the content of a mission. The goods in question, life
goods, destiny determining goods, are matters not in the first place
of my choice, but of God's choice for me. It is a matter of the mission he gives, and gives in freedom. So, no, not everyone is obliged
to be chaste and poor and obedient in the religious life. Nor is every
man obliged to seek ordination. The good of marriage does not
automatically oblige the embrace of it. Rather, in all cases, the great
good of sharing in God's will trumps every other good.

In this way, too, by an attention to mission, there is solved the
question that arises apropos of the traditional distinction between
commandment and counsel. All must keep the two commandments
of love, but only some are called to the evangelical life. How, Hans
Urs von Balthasar asks, can obedience to the commandments of
love not include that "best" of the evangelical life that imitates the
Lord? And if I am called, invited by God to such a life, am I really
free to turn it down? As to the first question, what I most am bound
to is the will of God, his mission for me, and he does not call all to
the evangelical state, and not every mission is contained in the life
of the counsels. And for the second question, I may be free to turn
down a mission, but not without wounding love. The call to the
religious life is a very great good, and it obliges just as such.
Whether one sins in turning it down can be disputed.[15]

Perhaps we do not often speak today of an obligation to marry.
Someone would think we are speaking of "dynastic responsibilities"
or of a boy doing his duty to his pregnant girlfriend. Some are happy
to think that the arrival of the pill has made the second reference as
historical as the passing of kings has the first. That there is an obligation to marry makes perfect sense, however, if we pay attention to
the goods of marriage. Evidently, this obligation depends not only

---

[15] See Balthasar, *Christian State,* 32–40, for the discussion of obligation and
counsel apropos of the religious life; 493–505, on rejection of the call.

on the goods that I perceive and that call to me, but also on the perception and willingness of my prospective partner. Other things being equal, however, once a man and woman are willing to marry, and see the good of marrying each other, then the obligation is there. This is why Trollope's Lily Dale rightly bears the opprobrium she does for refusing the offer of Johnny Eames in *The Small House at Allington* and *The Last Chronicle of Barset*. She *should* have married Johnny, and everyone sees it. What can this "should" mean but that there is in some sense an obligation to the goods of marriage—particular goods—and even before one says "I do"?

The question of mutual will for marriage is not dissimilar to the question of mutual will for religious vows. For religious vows, many wills must be in concord: first, God's and the novice's, but we should also include those of the authorities ecclesiastical. For marriage, the spouses must be in concord. If we follow the path marked out by John Paul II, we shall certainly include God's will as calling the couple to marriage. And then for marriage there are the wills of the authorities both civil and ecclesiastical.

What the wills must be in concord about is some good, some good to be targeted, embraced, accomplished, lived in the life that is entered into by promise. Both the religious and married states of life, as well as the priesthood, find their norm and model in Christ. It is by looking at him that we see the good at stake, the good as religiously, Christianly determined.

First, the evangelical life is founded by him who had nowhere to lay his head, who was the first of the eunuchs for the sake of the Kingdom of God, who was obedient to his Father unto death. Next, the priesthood is a participation in his priesthood, consummated at his death. Finally, he is the Spouse of the Church, who is the bride of the Lamb. As such, he enables a renewed marriage, one restored to the pattern of the beginnings, where what God puts together man does not put asunder.

It is worth noting with Balthasar that the evangelical life of the Lord is foundational and normative for the other two states.[16] That

---

[16] Ibid., 133–62, 183–200.

is, the priestly act of Christ, his sacrifice, is imbued with his obedience unto death, just as it is at the same time the ultimate dispossession of his body in virtue of which many are enriched. This same priestly act is at the same time the virginal making fecund of the womb of the Church and the washing of the bride in the bath of regeneration, and so lays down a pattern for marriage of mutual obedience (Eph 5:21, 25–27).

It is no accident, furthermore, that the manifestation of the states is temporally distended. First, our Lord, obedient to his mission, lives the evangelical life of poverty and chastity. Second, only at the consummation of his life, on the cross, does he exercise his priesthood. And third, it is only in glory that he is fully constituted as the Spouse of the Church. He may be designated Bridegroom before that (for example at Cana, Jn 2, Mt 9:15, Mt 25:1), but the consummation of the nuptials is eschatological. In this way, what one might suppose, and with reason, to be the most earthly of the states is ordered to and becomes a sign of the new heavens and the new earth.

If in each case there is response to a call, for marriage or priesthood or religious life, there here comes to light the further good, that of sharing in the choice of God, the choice God makes for each one of us.[17] It is in this way especially that we enact our friendship with God, trusting him to have chosen the best thing for us.   ⁘

---

[17] Balthasar, *Christian State,* 400–401: "whoever shares, by his obedience to mission, in this truth and freedom of God, shares also in the choice, the plans and the providence of God himself."

chapter twenty-two
Marriage Pagan and Christian

THE CONTRAST of pagan and Christian priesthood is a contrast of a shadow to the reality. Even Old Testament priesthood is but a type of the reality, the priesthood of Christ, in which Christians participate in different ways by baptism and orders. There is more continuity between pagan marriage and Christian marriage, however. As we have already noted, marriage and marriage promises make sense prior to and outside of Christianity. They do not make altogether the same sense, however, and this a function of the goods involved.

In the Latin Catholic West, Christian marriage has been understood to be indissoluble. That is, if separation of bed and board has been countenanced in cases of extreme marital breakdown, and if in that sense divorce has been countenanced, it was never recognized that the marriage bond itself could be dissolved such as to permit remarriage.[1] There is a contrast to be drawn with the modern understanding of divorce; there is also a contrast to be drawn with ancient, pre-Christian acceptance of divorce and remarriage.

If the obligation of promising is a function of the promised good, then the destruction of the good, or the impossibility of the

---

[1] St. Augustine, *Adulterous Marriages,* Book I, 5.5 and 6.6, in *Marriage and Virginity,* trans. Ray Kearney, *The Works of Saint Augustine: A Translation of the 21st Century,* ed. John Rotelle (Hyde Park, NY: New City Press, 1999), I/9, 145. The discipline of the Eastern Church, as of the churches of the Reformation, is of course different.

realization of the good, renders a promise null and void. So, trivially, if I promise to take you to the arcade next Tuesday, I am relieved of the obligation if the arcade is destroyed by fire on Monday. There is no longer an arcade to which to take you, and the good in question, namely, the entertainment of precisely that afternoon at the arcade is no longer possible of realization. Nontrivially, ancient Roman practice permitted a man to divorce his wife for barrenness, and the *lex Iulia* of Augustus *required* a man to divorce an adulterous wife.[2] Remarriage was permitted. Saving the more privileged position of the husband, which it is not my purpose to consider, such divorce and remarriage seems entirely reasonable. The good of children and the good of having an heir to which to leave one's property in orderly fashion being impossible of realization, or the good of friendship within marriage being precluded or irrecoverable, the promises are dissolved.[3] In the high imperial era, furthermore, where mutual consent was taken to establish marriage, so the will of either of the parties sufficed for divorce.[4]

We have just mentioned two of the traditional goods of marriage recognized by St. Augustine. And we have just adverted to the consent that the common theology of marriage calls the "form" of the sacrament, the sacramental sign supplied by the spouses themselves in making the marriage. In Christian marriage, as in pre-Christian marriage, there can be barrenness and sterility. In Christian as in pre-Christian marriage, there can be such breakdown of friendship that any reasonable observer would say it is irrecoverable. Why do Christians not dissolve their marriages, therefore, as did the reasonable Romans? Again, in Christian as in Roman marriage, mutual consent

---

[2] Jane F. Gardner, *Women in Roman Law and Society* (Bloomington, IN: Indiana University Press, 1986), 81, 89–90.

[3] Captivity of a spouse was not considered divorce, but was taken to dissolve a marriage; see Philip Lyndon Reynolds, *Marriage in the Western Church: The Christianization of Marriage during the Patristic and Early Medieval Periods* (Leiden: E. J. Brill, 1994), 44.

[4] Gardner, *Women*, 81, 86; Reynolds, *Marriage*, 46f. See Edward Schillebeeckx, *Marriage: Human Reality and Saving Mystery* (London: Sheed and Ward, 1965), 241.

makes the marriage. How then could it be equally strong to unmake it for the Romans, but not for Christians?

The answer to the first question is in what St. Augustine recognized as another good in Christian marriage beyond offspring and beyond fidelity or friendship. This good is the bond itself. In contrast to the bond that just any marriage is, a bond in service to the goods of children and friendship, the bond of Christian marriage was special, and made for Augustine a third good in addition to, coordinate with, the other two, the "sacramental bond," a symbol of the union of Christ and the Church.[5] Marriage as signing and sharing in the reality of the union of Christ and the Church is what the Latin Catholic West has taken to give intelligibility to the prohibition of divorce. It is the ground, as it were, of the Lord's legislation of Matthew 19. This bond of marriage still serves the goods of children and marriage and stable society, but it is not something purely instrumental to these goods. It can itself be picked out as a distinct good of the same or even greater weight, as it were, than the others.

St. Augustine's terminology bears closer inspection. Why does he call this third good of marriage the "sacrament"? In the first place, as Philip L. Reynolds points out, *sacramentum* belongs to the semantic field expressing oaths and pledges. "In particular, *sacramentum* denoted the military oath of allegiance and by extension the obligation consequent upon the oath."[6] Even before Augustine, Lactantius and St. Ambrose are seen to speak of marriage "as a *sacramentum* in the sense of a vowed bond."[7] Second, there was the translation of *mysterion* in Ephesians 5:31–32 by *sacramentum*.[8] St.

---

[5] The "sacramental bond" is the marriage bond of a "sacramental" marriage; it is the marriage bond between two baptized Christians. For the symbolism, see St. Augustine, *The Excellence of Marriage*, 18.21, in *Marriage and Virginity*, trans. Ray Kearney, *The Works of Saint Augustine: A Translation of the 21st Century*, ed. John Rotelle (Hyde Park, NY: New City Press, 1999), I/9, 49, and for the bond itself directly, *Excellence*, 24.32, (45), and *Adulterous Marriages* II, 4–5, (167–69). Schillebeeckx's discussion in *Marriage*, 281–86, is good, but Reynolds, *Marriage*, 280–311, is much more comprehensive and satisfying.

[6] Reynolds, *Marriage*, 282.

[7] Ibid.

[8] Ibid., 282–93.

Paul first quotes Genesis 2:24, "For this reason a man shall leave his father and mother and be joined to his wife, and the two shall become one flesh," and then continues: "This mystery [*mysterion, sacramentum*] is a profound one, and I am saying that it refers to Christ and the church." The scripture from Genesis according to which the Lord teaches the indissolubility of marriage in Matthew 19:6 prophetically (mysteriously) refers to the union of Christ and the Church, and the union of Christ and the Church itself is another way of speaking of the "mystery which is Christ in you, the hope of glory" (Col 1:27). This mystery is the plan of God, now revealed, to unite all things in Christ (Eph 1:10), the mystery into which St. Paul has such insight (Eph 3:4) and according to which he sees that Jews and Gentiles are to form one body of Christ (Eph 3:6), the body that is the bride of 5:32. So, the sacrament that is the vowed bond of the spouses makes us think of the sacrament of the union of Christ and the Church.

Additionally, as Reynolds points out, there is the fact that St. Augustine had already used *sacramentum* to refer to the "abiding sacrament" of baptism and orders, that is, the effect of those sacraments that remains even under the conditions of apostasy or schism and later called the "character" of these sacraments.[9] And baptism is evoked just prior to Ephesians 5:31–32, at verse 26, where Christ is said by his passion and death to wash his bride, the Church, in the laver that is at once the wedding bath and the bath of baptism.[10] Just as the first washing of baptism effects a permanent relation to the Church and so to Christ, so marriage, evoked by the wedding bath, effects something permanent too.

It is hard to say what this bond is, but it is more than a reality of the moral order, of the "acquired rights and obligations" of the partners, for as Reynolds points out, even when the marriage "fails," there is something—*quiddam coniugale*—that remains, a holy bond

---

[9] Ibid., 282.

[10] See Reynolds's discussion, ibid., 293–97. The phrase "abiding sacrament" is from Colman O'Neill, *Sacramental Realism* (Princeton, NJ: Scepter Publishers, 1998), 128ff.

that prevents remarriage.[11] The bond both signifies the unbreakable union of Christ and the Church, and so must itself be permanent to do so, and as well is a sort of participation in this marriage, the marriage par excellence of Christ and his bride. The great mystery, the great sacrament, is that of Christ and the Church, and the little sacraments, the little marriages of Christian spouses, are participations of it.[12] So much can the entire economy of salvation be seen in nuptial terms, moreover, that Augustine likens the Scriptures to the *tabulae matrimoniales* or *nupitiales* of Roman marriage. These documents specified the content of the marriage contract, and so identified what "husband" and "wife" meant. So, Augustine has it, speaking of the Gospels:

> That's how the sacred reading of the gospel, year after year, points out to us the true Christ and the true Church, to make sure we are not mistaken in either of them, by introducing the wrong bride to the holy bridegroom, or by presenting the holy bride with someone other than her true husband. So, to be sure we make no mistake about either of them, let us listen, as it were, to their marriage lines [the *tabulae*] in the gospel.[13]

And in this sermon, Luke 24 is used to identify Christ as the truly incarnate Son dead and risen, and the bride as the universal Church who preaches him throughout the world.

As a participation in the great sacrament of Christ and the Church, the little sacrament of matrimony is a sharing in the goods of salvation, a specification of Christian sharing in the holiness of the Church and the redemptive action of Christ that makes the Church holy. As Reynolds says:

---

[11] Reynolds, *Marriage,* 298–99.

[12] Ibid., 289, 291–92

[13] St. Augustine, Sermon 238.1, in *Sermons,* vol. 7, *(230–272B) on the Liturgical Seasons,* trans. Edmund Hill, OP, *The Works of Saint Augustine: A Translation of the 21st Century,* ed. John Rotelle (Hyde Park, NY: New City Press, 1990), III/7, 56. See on this and similar passages David G. Hunter, "Augustine and the Making of Marriage in Roman North Africa," *Journal of Early Christian Studies* 11 (2003): 82–83.

> marriage does more than signify the mystical union [of Christ
> and the Church], if by "signify " one means the kind of relation
> that obtains, for example, between a crucifix and an the Cross of
> Christ. It emulates and in some way embodies it.[14]

Which is to say, in a later idiom of sacramental theology, that marriage is a sacrament that gives grace. The consent of the vows signifies the bond, and the bond signifies the grace by which Christ saves
the Church in uniting it to himself as his bride and body.

> [Augustine] asks his readers to think of marriage in terms of the
> mystical marriage in which all Christians participate and which is
> the archetype of Christian marriage.[15]

Christian marriage is thus a further determination of the way in
which baptismal grace, making us one with Christ—his body, his
bride—operates for all Christians. Within Christian marriage, the
bond is both sign and instrument: as a sign of Christ's union with
the Church, it is the instrument he uses to keep these members of
the Church, the married couple, united to him in grace.

There is still the question of the impotence of the mutual consent of Christians to dissolve a marriage. Part of the answer is that
the consent of Christians in marriage is merely an instrument in a
way that outside of Christian marriage it is not. The principal agent
of the sacraments, marriage included, is Christ. In marriage, he uses
the sacramental sign—here, the exchange of consent—to make the
sacramental bond, that third good recognized by Augustine. Husband and wife are spoken of as "what God has put together" in
Matthew 19, and this means not just that the institution of marriage is established in the beginning by God, but that God through
Christ puts each Christian couple together.

The bond is unbreakable, therefore, for two reasons. First, it is
the sign of the unbreakable bond between Christ and the Church.
Christian marriage could not be the good it is, therefore, without
being indissoluble. Second, it is a bond established by Christ. And

---

[14] Reynolds, *Marriage*, 300.
[15] Ibid., 301.

what Christ does on behalf of the God who puts husband and wife together, no man who wishes to put asunder can undo.

Let us return to the point of departure of this chapter. For our purposes, what is formal to the comparison of pagan and Christian marriage is this, namely, that both pagan and Christian marriage, pagan and Christian promising, look to certain goods. The difference in the permanence of the relation, and the difference in resolution with which marriage is entered into and maintained, are functions of the difference between goods that both pagans and Christians can recognize, on the one hand, and on the other, a good that only Christians can see since it can be seen only by faith and realized in faith's household. The bond as sign of and way of realizing the relation between Christ and the Church is a good of an order beyond any that the pagans could know, fashioned by an agent beyond any agent of this world. Even as to the goods Christian and pagan marriage recognize in common, moreover, it must be that Christianity makes Christian spouses behold them in a new light. Children are destined not just to be citizens of the world but citizens of heaven, and the friendship of the spouses is a form of Christian charity.

On the other hand, the contrast of what marriage is for Christians and what it is for modernity involves something more than a recognition of different goods. The more basic issue here is different accounts of binding. For Christians and pagans, the good binds. For moderns, the will, never itself bound, binds. But if for both pagans and Christians, we can recognize the good as binding, for as long as the good exists, for both pagans and moderns we can see that the spouses alone are involved in making the marriage. There is no consent but their own fashioning the marriage. For Christians, things are more complex: marriage involves them in transcendent goods, and while it is not fashioned without their agency, it is not fashioned by their agency alone. Religion, for the pagans, was in service to a this-worldly reality. Christian marriage hallows a this-worldly reality, but it does so by making it participate in a reality altogether beyond the world.

The seeming harshness of the Roman Church's discipline regarding marriage and divorce is strictly parasitic on the good she thinks to perceive in marriage. This strictness could be mitigated only by supposing Christian marriage is not as good as once was thought. Even when the marriage does fail according to all earthly hope and measure, the bond remains as a divine sign, a divine pledge of grace to him or her who would receive it, and as a sign, for those who would not, of the God who stretches out his hands to a sinful nation.

But since the principal agent of the marriage bond is Christ, who has resources for reconciliation and for healing human beings beyond the human, it is more difficult, because less reasonable, to give up all hope for Christian marriages in trouble. For the same reason that Christians cannot ever give up hope for the salvation of any man, a married Christian cannot ever give up hope for his or her spouse. The hope is not in the power of the human heart to heal itself, but in the power of Christ to pluck out the heart of stone and insert the heart of flesh. It is not a hope that "time will heal all wounds," for we know it does not. It is a hope that Eternity in time may heal all wounds because of the wounds of Christ.   ⋮⋮

chapter twenty-three

:::: Christian Vows
:::: Dispensable and Indispensable

CHRISTIAN MARRIAGE is indissoluble because it is Christian, and Christian marriage vows indispensable because they are Christian. Why does the Christian character of promising to be a religious or celibate priest not similarly make for indispensability? This question, too, leads to a consideration of the goods involved in each case.

Marriage is a sacrament. The bond of Christian marriage—each marriage—is established by Christ, as has been said. The vow of obedience or the promise of celibacy, on the other hand, is not made by Christ but by the monk or nun or priest. We can say, if we want, that as something created, the vow or the promise is made more by God than by the created person who makes it. Because plants are created, God is more responsible for the sugar in the beet than the beet is. In the same way, if my vowing poverty and chastity is not sinful, he is more responsible in every respect for my vowing than I am. In religious promising, however, and however much I may hope to be doing God's will, he nonetheless does not appear in his own name as guarantor for what is promised. It is the same with swearing. When I swear to the truth of something, we may say that God is more responsible for the display of what is true than I am. Even though I swear by him and his power to requite liars, however, he does not stand forth in his own voice as guaranteeing the truth of what is said. In religious promising as in swearing, I am the one who is seen to take responsibility for keeping the promise and telling the truth, not God. In other words, it is not like God promising through the mouth of Moses or swearing through the mouth of Jeremiah. So, if the intelligibility and goodness of the vow are in fact the declaration because the display of the divine mind and will, they are not immediately presented to be known as God's display of them. The only responsibility they engage with certainty is my responsibility, the truth of my practical intelligence and the freedom of my will.

By contrast, sacramental action is the immediate manifestation of the mind and will of Christ because it is his action. It is his action, moreover, not simply as God and in virtue of the divine agency, but more precisely as man, acting through his human nature. Sacramental action is manifestly his action, and as principal agent of the sacraments, in such a way that the action of the ministers is merely instrumental. The promise of priest or religious, though it presupposes both the divine call and the grace to answer it, is not similarly instrumental in this way to the action of Christ. The only person manifestly engaged for fulfillment is the human person, not God or Christ.

Marriage is complicated. Marriage is made by the vows of the spouses, which vows are the immediate manifestation of their minds and wills and engage them to fulfill the promises. At the same time, these vows are part of the sacrament. In marriage, the vows that bespeak the minds and hearts of the betrothed are also and in addition taken immediately as speaking the mind and heart of Christ, as willing this couple to be married, and as willing their married bond to be the sign of his own relation to the Church. The vows of the spouses enter into the action of Christ as his instrument, by which he effects both the bond of marriage and the grace of the sacrament. Just like the character of baptism, therefore, the bond is the immediate effect of the action of Christ, and just as little can it be undone by the human power of human persons. As the character of baptism, the permanent effect of baptism, forbids rebaptism, so the marriage bond forbids remarriage. What is exclusively bound to one cannot be bound to another. On the other hand, what the vows of religious or the promises of priestly celibacy effect, since it is not an effect of a divine agent, may be more revocable than marriage vows.

We might put things as follows. Christ calls whom he chooses to the evangelical life. But the promising of a religious is not in and of itself Christ's action for the salvation of the one who promises. Such saving action of Christ is more a response to the promise that the promise itself. But the promises of marriage are in and of themselves Christ's action for the salvation of those who marry. So to speak, God has promised to be the principal agent of the marriage promises the spouses make; God has not similarly promised to be the principal agent of the promises religious make. God has promised to make the promises of the spouses always and in every case a means to salvation. He has not promised always and in every case to make religious promises a means to salvation. This difference can be captured by saying that marriage is a sacrament and religious profession is not. This difference is captured by saying that marriage, like every sacrament, is efficacious of grace *ex opere operato*, and the religious profession is efficacious *ex opere operantis*. In this respect, religious profession is more risky.

In speaking of the vows of religious and priests, St. Thomas likens a vow to a private law, and says that vows can be dispensed for the same reason we can be granted exceptions to the letter of the law in circumstances where keeping it would do more harm than good or be simply evil.[1] In other words, a dispensation is like an exercise of *epikeia*; it is a taking account of the intention of the legislator in circumstances he did not foresee.[2] So, St. Thomas holds, the promise of priestly celibacy can be dispensed. It is not essentially connected with holy orders, but connected to it, if very fittingly so, only by institution of the Church.[3] On the other hand, marriage vows are not dispensed because of "the good of the sacrament."[4]

---

[1] *Summa theologiae* II–II, Q. 88, a. 10, c.
[2] *Summa theologiae* II–II, Q. 120, a. 1, c.
[3] *Summa theologiae* II–II, Q. 88, a. 10, c.
[4] *Summa theologiae* Suppl., Q. 67, a. 1, ad 2.

Now St. Thomas held in addition that religious vows—the vows by which one became a monk—were indispensable.[5] The gift of self to God by way of the vows could not be retrieved, as it were, by any earthly or even ecclesiastical power. Made by man, they were nevertheless received by God. There was a kind of untouchable quality to religious life, just as there was to marriage. You could get yourself into it, but no power on earth could get you out of it. Entering into religious life used to have the same sort of irrevocability, the same sense of burning bridges behind, that marriage did and according to law still does. This discipline was maintained until the promulgation of the Code of Canon Law of 1918, which provides for dispensation from solemn vows. This provision is maintained in the new Code of 1983.[6]

How should we think of this change? We should think of the goods involved in the promises. It is they that govern the dispensability or indispensability of the promises. There are three ways to get at this.

In the first place, celibacy, as well as poverty and obedience, are renunciations. Obedience is a renunciation of autonomy, poverty of ownership. Celibacy is a renunciation of marriage, which includes a renunciation of goods of the orders of both nature and grace. The goods of marriage, of property, of the free disposition of one's affairs are put aside in order to respond more single-mindedly to the love of God, to the work of "pleasing the Lord," as St. Paul puts it (1 Cor 7). Marriage, on the other hand, is not a renunciation, but a taking up of goods, a response to and a possession of the quite determinate goods of children and friendship and fidelity and the bond. Because the foundation of religious promising is a renunciation of goods, it is dispensable without attacking those goods. Moreover, the dispensation from a renunciation of goods is not a direct attack on the goods for the sake of which the renunciation was undertaken but aims at the restoration of the renounced goods. The dispensation of mar-

---

[5] *Summa theologiae* II–II, Q. 88, a. 10, c. Lafont, *Imagining the Catholic Church*, 12–121, 131–32, suggests a return to this view.

[6] Canon 692.

riage vows, on the contrary, would touch the very goods the vows respond to and is no restoration of a lost good.

Second, we should recall the old way in which the religious life was conceived. For it will be observed, granted the renunciations religious make, they are responding to goods, very great goods, just as are married people. Why does not dispensing them "touch" these goods, as dispensation from marriage would attack or denigrate the goods of marriage? The goods built upon the renunciation of the vows are things like greater spiritual freedom and, for ministers, greater pastoral freedom and a superior concentration of focus on the affairs of the Lord and how to please him. These things are something real. How does dispensation not destroy them?

The answer is that it of course does, but also these goods have a certain character of means to an end. Writing in the fifth century, John Cassian explained that the final end of the monk is the kingdom of God, and that the monk attains this by aiming at purity of heart.[7] It is for the sake of purity of heart, moreover, that one renounces wealth.[8] Poverty, the renunciation of wealth, is a means to an end. Cassian further explains that renunciations of marriage and wealth serve to the renunciation of vice, itself a step on the way to the renunciation of all visible and earthly things.[9] Priestly celibacy, for its part, is a means to greater pastoral charity. These means, moreover, while singularly effective, are not the absolutely unique way to attaining the relevant ends. Purity of heart, in other words, is still attainable "in the world." To renounce these means is by no means to renounce the end and, in certain circumstances, may be necessary for the sake of the end.[10] Again by contrast, the goods of marriage are not so to be characterized. Children, and friendship, and the

---

[7] John Cassian, *The Conferences,* trans. Boniface Ramsey, OP, Ancient Christian Writers 57 (New York: Paulist Press, 1997), First Conference: On the goal and the end of the monk, III, 42, and IV.3, 43.

[8] Ibid., V.3, 44.

[9] Ibid., Third Conference: On the three renunciations, VII.1–2, 124–25. Cassian himself would not apply this distinction of end and means so radically as is done today; see the Seventeenth Conference: On making promises, XVIII, 611.

[10] Bernard Häring, *The Law of Christ,* II (Cork: Mercier Press, 1963), 293–94.

marriage bond itself as a sign and promise of grace for rearing children and keeping marital friendship are rather more terminal than the goods that make up the vowed life.

In the third place, religious vows constitute a way of life that is more an anticipation of a heavenly fullness and reality than a participation in it. The virginal state of heaven, where no one marries and no one is given in marriage, is a participation in the Good incomparably beyond that of earthly marriage.[11] On earth, however, virginal or celibate enjoyment of created goods is less than that of marriage. Now, we can obliterate an anticipation of eschatological goods without obliterating what is anticipated. But the breaking of marriage vows involves the destruction of quite real goods here and now. Christian marriage is an anticipation in its own way of the *eschaton*, but it is more than that, because founded on quite this-worldly goods, that although taken up into the supernatural order, and even precisely because so taken up, cannot be attacked.

In divorce and remarriage of Christians, moreover, there is a sort of denial of the truthfulness of the marriage vows, and of the validity of the exercise of the practical intelligence and freedom of the both spouses. If this exercise really does serve to make an indissoluble bond, then the attempt to dispense is a saying that the thing never happened. Dispensation collapses into a declaration of nullity. In dispensation of religious, there is no declaration that the promises were not made and validly. The possibility of the dispensation depends on the different status of the goods involved.

How, finally, should we think of the suspension of a priest and his release from episcopal obedience? This is most similar to separation of bed and board for married people. In neither case is the sacrament denied. But the exercise of the priesthood and the exercise of married life are suspended for the good of persons. Priestly promises, however, deserve a word unto themselves.

---

[11] John Paul II, *Theology of the Body,* 238, 244–45.

::: *chapter twenty-four*
::: Priestly Promises

I N MARRIAGE, we say, Christ uses the promises of the spouses to make a Christian marriage, an image of and participation in the marriage of Christ and the Church. In entering religious life, a man or woman makes promises to God, although these promises are not themselves promised instruments of Christ in quite the same way the promises are in marriage. In ordination, Christ is once again the principal agent, as in marriage. On the other hand, there is no promise that enters into the very making of the priest in the rite of ordination, as there is in the making of both married people and the religious life. Valid ordination permanently makes a man radically capable of acting as a priest, whether or not the priest intends or has promised to live as a priest until death.

In fact, priests do promise to be priests for life—rather obscurely, it must be said. Where is this done? We can see it more or less implicit in the liturgy of ordination. Just prior to his ordination to the diaconate, the candidate who is destined for priesthood makes a public promise of celibacy. However, this is rather a requirement of the legal than the sacramental order just as such. It is a requirement of great pastoral and spiritual fittingness, but not one built into the structure of the sacrament just as such. And yet it would be difficult to understand the figure of the priest did we not know that, in addition to the promise of celibacy, he is also understood to promise to be a priest—to conform his life to Christ, to give himself over in charity to the pastoral ministry. This promise finds some expression in his public promise of obedience to the bishop, since it is a promise to obey as a priest, in the pastoral ministry, and there is no further limit placed on this obedience. So, it is an obedience for as long as the priest is alive. This promise finds further expression in the interrogation of the candidate during the rite: "Are you resolved to consecrate your life to God for the salvation of his people?" Consecration of life bespeaks a temporal wholeness. The candidate promises to be a priest his whole life for the good of the people of God. There is also an expression of this temporal wholeness engaged in priesthood in the prayers and in the action of the rite itself, and perhaps, after all, this is the best place for it to come to expression. So, in the litany, we pray simply that God "consecrate" the candidate for his "sacred duties," and that is a very capacious prayer indeed. The anointing with oil, too, bespeaks a sort of permanent alteration of the anointed, one that we expect to see displayed in the course of the priest's whole life.

Outside the liturgy, however, the Roman Church arranges for a very express and clear promise to be a priest for one's life. Canon 1036 provides that, in addition to declaring his freedom in seeking orders, the candidate also testify "that he will devote himself perpetually to the ecclesiastical ministry."

Why is the ordination rite so laconic, so circumspect about so important a matter, that, as it were, law must come to the aid of liturgy? We must first ask why a man should want to be and why we should want him to want to be a priest his whole life.

Is it good that a man be a priest and promise to be a priest his whole life? It seems that a temporary priesthood is easy enough to conceive. Within the last thirty years, it has been thought that the Church might ask a man to be a priest for ten years or so and then, so to speak, release him for normal life. Just so, we can think of part-time priests, too.[1] Especially in some rural situations, or where congregations are very small and can scarcely either support a priest or

---

[1] See, for example, Raymond Hickey, *A Case for an Auxiliary Priesthood* (Maryknoll, NY: Orbis Books, 1982).

occupy all his energies, this might seem to make sense. There is something objectively unfitting about both proposals, however. It is an unfittingness that comes from the nature of the goods that priests respond to and embrace and are empowered to serve by ordination.

In the first place, there is an unfittingness about part-time priesthood. The priest is one sent, even as the apostles before him, by Christ, and even as Christ by the Father. The priest is an ambassador and representative of Christ. "Being sent" as a representative of one whose mission, whose whole life, was the complete and adequate expression of his Person fittingly calls for a full-time commitment to such representation. But that is the good, the representation of Christ, the priest embraces. The completeness of the priest's engagement in discharging priestly functions is a sign both of the Person in whose name these functions are discharged and of the completeness with which the humanity of this Person was given over to his teaching, ruling, and sanctifying mission.

Moreover, if we want to think about these functions more particularly, then it must be said that preaching, sanctifying, ruling are capable of engaging all of one's energies and time. That they do so is a witness to the unsurpassable importance of their successful exercise for the people for whom they are exercised. Ministry in charity and wisdom to the Body of Christ that is the Church is certainly capable of absorbing all of the priest's energies; it is objectively worthy of that; and in the Western Church this is fittingly signified and lived out in the "full-time" character of priestly ministry. It is therefore fitting as well that the daily bread of the priest be granted him in virtue of his entire dedication to these his "functions."[2]

One can think of it as a matter of seriousness. Really important things, serious things, absorb a man's energy and time. Human society is structured by the division of labor, and the divisions indicate the amount of labor, or the kind of eminent level of skill and expertise, or both, needed to perform some service or produce some good. The priesthood ought not to be a hobby.

---

2 See *Presbyterorum ordinis*, 20.

This means that, while priests may perforce and according to circumstances have to do other things, and simply in order to support themselves, the "other things" will be, and will be experienced as, a distraction. Radically, the prophetic task should consume one; as a matter of the heart, there can be no "part-time" or "half-time" priests, and ordinarily and for the most part, this will be translated into a quite visible and manifest singleness of occupation.[3]

In this light, realizing that the priest is a representative of Christ, we can see why it should be that the promise to be a priest should find the kind of indirect expression it does in the rite, and why the liturgy is so laconic about this. Married people must choose each other, albeit Christ uses this choice to make their marriage an image of his own relation to the Church. But a priest does not choose to represent Christ. That is, he is not the original and principal person who so chooses. In general, the one who is represented rather has the initiative in choosing who will represent him. And this is supereminently so in this case. A man does not choose to be a priest so much as he is chosen. "He called to himself those whom he desired . . . ; and he appointed twelve, to be with him and to be sent out" (Mk 3:13–14). And again, "You did not choose me, but I chose you and appointed you that you should go and bear fruit" (Jn 15:16). Doubtless, this initiative is to be freely ratified by the one called.

Doubtless, too, this ratification must engage the whole life of the priest. Just as the priest's work is full time, so it is for all the time of his life. Priesthood is by its nature not a career one can finish; it is not a yoke one can fittingly take on and then put off. Since the word he preaches claims the whole of the existence of those he preaches to, the whole of the preacher's existence must show that the wager of one's life on the truth of the Gospel can be made. For temporally conditioned man, this means the wager is to be expressed in the whole of one's life. The claim on one's entire existence will be a claim on one's entire temporal existence such that priests will be expected to be priests, that is, to act and function as priests, for their

---

[3] These brief remarks should not be taken to settle anything about the French "worker-priests" of the last century.

entire lives, and it will be scandalous, in the Gospel sense of that word, for someone to "leave the priesthood." We can say, too, that the publicity of the word the priest preaches calls for a similarly public declaration of the extent of its claim, and this he does by promising celibacy, and by being a priest for life.

Finally, it is to be observed that preaching the Gospel, and service to both the *corpus Christi verum* (Eucharist) and *corpus Christi mysticum* (Church) are not "functions" that can be discharged in abstraction from one's person. Some functions claim only part of a person's talents, and can be discharged without any serious commitment of the heart to their intrinsic worth and importance. But this is not so with regard to the functions of a priest. The word that he is charged to preach to those to whom he is sent, and that is supposed to engage their whole heart and mind and strength, claiming them wholly for the Lord, claims him, too, and he cannot therefore discharge this function without engaging himself in it at the deepest level of his heart, which is to say the level of that faith and hope and love that are the endowment of every Christian. The functions claim him entirely and for life, therefore, in much the same way that the office of husband or wife, in its own fashion, claims the whole of the persons who take them on. So also for sanctifying and governing. On the table of the Lord rests the Bread that he, too, lives by, and that is the Christian's sufficiency, beyond which we look for no other. And the community he serves by governing is the community in which his salvation, too, is to be worked out in fear and trembling. The priesthood is a plowshare one should not look back from once the hand is put to it.

chapter twenty-five

::: Promising and the Common
::: Good of the Church

QUESTIONS ABOUT the dispensability of vows suppose the role of authority in regulating promises and their fulfillment. The rulers of a community have such a role because promising touches on the common good of which the rulers have care. It is precisely in the common good, in fact, that John Finnis locates the obligation to keep promises:

> if that individual, like others, goes along with the practice [of promising] by trying to perform as he promised to perform, even when performance is at the expense of some inconvenience, foreseen or even unforeseen, to himself, he will thereby not only contribute to the well being of the person for whose benefit his promise was accepted . . . but will also be playing his part in a pattern of life without which many of the benefits of community could not in fact be realized.[1]

Beyond the immediate good promised, which we have emphasized, there is also the common good. Finnis specifies this as the good of individuals (their life, virtue, freedom, etc.), as well as the respect for individuals, the recognition of the good of individuals, that promise keeping shows.[2] Also, the common good includes such

---

[1] John Finnis, *Natural Law and Natural Rights* (New York: Oxford University Press, 1982), 306–7.
[2] Ibid., 305.

things as cooperation, predictability, and order.[3] In that sense of it, Finnis describes it as "the set of conditions which enables the members of a community . . . to realize reasonably for themselves the value(s), for the sake of which they have reason to collaborate with each other . . . in a community."[4]

If we say that we collaborate with each other in the Church for the sake of becoming permanent and eternal members of the Heavenly City, and being even now brothers and sisters with one another because brothers and sisters first of Christ and so sons and daughters of God, we know that this working with one another is founded on God's prior working in us. The good order of our collaboration in Christ is one of the chief components of the common good of the Church. It is an order of charity, whose principle is the Holy Spirit.

The good of order can be broken down into several components. Bernard Lonergan picks out five: persons, intellectual and moral virtues, the exercise of these virtues, "the succession and series of particular goods," and interpersonal relations. Persons need many things, but individuals are not sufficient unto themselves to provide the requisite series of goods. The operations by which we seek and attain these goods for ourselves and others are the exercises of the virtues. Last, there is this:

> since knowers and willers both acquire habits and perform operations ordered among themselves, as well as distribute the available particular goods among themselves, they will the good of order both for themselves as well as for others; but to wish good to someone is to love him; the effect of love, however, is that union and mutual inherence which is best among personal relations; and therefore, the human good of order brings about interpersonal relations.[5]

---

[3] Ibid., 303.

[4] Ibid., 155.

[5] Bernard Lonergan, *De Deo Trino*, II: *Pars systematica seu Divinarum personarum conceptio analogica* (Rome: Gregorian University Press, 1964), 245. Lonergan appeals to *Summa theologiae* I, Q. 20, a. 1, ad 3, and I–II, Q. 28, aa. 1 and 2, for his remarks on love.

Moreover, there is a certain preeminence to the role of interpersonal relations:

> For we want to share goods with those whom we love; we willingly cooperate with them so that they may become good; we acquire the necessary habits and hate the opposed defects the more efficacious is the cooperation; and therefore, if the union of love is given, there follow the other things that make the good of order, as is seen most of all in matrimony.[6]

Evidently, the good of order both contributes to and is fostered by interpersonal relations, that is, friendly relations.

If we turn to think about the good of order in the community of the Church, we shall list Persons, namely Christ and the Holy Spirit and all who are in Christ by the Spirit, the supernatural virtues of faith and hope and charity and the infused moral virtues, the exercise of these virtues, and the succession and series of particular goods. These goods are to be understood:

> according to the fruit which new life in Christ perpetually brings, according to the ministry of the word by which the Gospel is preached to every creature, according to the ministry of life which is discerned in sacrifice, priesthood, sacraments, and as well according to the hierarchy which orders and perfects the Church.[7]

The role of personal relations maintains its preeminence:

> Finally, there are personal relations, since Christians love one another just as Christ has loved them (Jn 15:12, 13:34), and loving one another love Christ (Mt 25:31–46), and loving Christ are loved by the Father (Jn 14:21; 16:27), and to them by the Father through Christ is sent the Holy Spirit (Jn 14:15ff.).[8]

Now, if we engage to supply these goods to one another in the Church through the promises of marriage and priesthood and religious life,

---

6 Ibid., 246.

7 Ibid., 247.

8 Ibid.

then promises evidently have a central role, as we should expect, in the common good of the Church, and this common good of the Church gives occasion for these same promises. Other things being equal, the common good of the Church is a greater common good than that of the earthly community, and so the obligation of religious promises is greater. Baptismal promising inserts us into the economy of the great corporation of the Church, than which there is no more precious order. The further promising of marriage and religious life and priesthood inserts us more particularly into that same economy. Promising unites us to the goods we embrace; it unites us to the community that prizes those goods and that depends on those goods being served; it is a central component in the maintenance of the order of this community. St. Augustine once called the Holy Spirit the glue of the Church. As involving us in the good of others and the common good, promising is a sort of analogue of the Holy Spirit. It is a sort of glue by which we find completion in being united to things and persons beyond ourselves; it is the binding of the members of the Church to one another and to their Head.

Our individual promises, in making the good order of the Church, help constitute the Church as herself the promise she is of the heavenly Jerusalem.   ::

::::: Epilogue

PROMISING—PROMISING something for life—looks at first to be one of those things that is a natural part of our natural lives. Christianity did not teach us how to promise, or introduce the very idea of promising into the human mind. Promising was there, all along, in the world of gods and men. If it was touched by divinity, it was a divinity that, like the humanity it dignified, was a part of the world. Promising for life, as in marriage, or at risk of one's life, as a warrior might in the heroic age, was something within the human scope. Men could do it; it made sense to them to do it; they did it without benefit of Christian clergy.

Although the practice of promising lived and prospered before the Gospel was preached, it is to be wondered whether promising will survive in the West anywhere else except under the protection of the Gospel.

There are other things like that, things that seemed human things, that flourished before the meeting of Athens and Jerusalem, before the intersection of Genesis and the *Timaeus*, but that do not seem able to collect themselves again and become whole once their embrace of Christianity loosens. Philosophy itself, at least in its form as a wisdom guiding life, seems to be one of them. Contemporary university philosophy has very little of the air of providing the practical wisdom that structures the whole of a human life. The sort of defense of human autonomy it undertakes—a defense of the freedom of indifference—prevents this. But pre-Christian philosophy was thoroughly oriented to the end of living the best and happy life, and supposed a battery of spiritual exercises for its practice.[1]

Promising may be another such thing that, having breathed a Christian air so long, cannot survive in the thinner atmosphere of modernity.

The pagan mind could keep alive a philosophy incomplete and riddled with *aporiai* but for that very reason open to a supernatural completion. But on the other side of the Middle Ages, once philosophy regained its independence, it pretended either to the completeness and closure and certitude that only theology could provide, as with Hegel, or it stultified itself and refused to look beyond the confines of the world or to admit a motion not absorbed by matter.[2] Maurice Blondel had a keen sense of this. "Is it not the case that we would will everything about God, except God Himself?" This he asks apropos of the "death of action," which includes the death of philosophy, once the claim of God has been refused.[3] The seed that does not fall into the earth and die does not remain forever; sooner or later it rots. "For to every one who has will more be given, and he will have abundance; but from him who has not, even what he has will be taken away" (Mt 25:29). This may be said fairly to define the relation of nature to grace for Blondel.[4]

Perhaps promising is one of the things that shall be taken away. If it really does make sense in the end only in relation to the good, and if the modern world banishes the good in order to create value, then promising is certainly one of those things.

Generally, the Christian story would give us to suppose that human things, natural things, are most clearly seen in divine light,

---

[1] Pierre Hadot, "Spiritual Exercises," in *Philosophy as a Way of Life*, ed. Arnold L. Davidson (Oxford: Blackwell, 2000).

[2] For the first alternative, see Mark Jordan, "The Terms of the Debate over "Christian Philosophy,'" *Communio* 12 (1985): 293–311.

[3] Maurice Blondel, *Action (1893): Essay on a Critique of Life and a Science of Practice,* trans. Oliva Blanchette (Notre Dame, IN: University of Notre Dame Press, 1984), 332. See Jordan, "Terms of the Debate."

[4] See his appeal to this verse in *The Letter on Apologetics*, trans. Alexander Dru and Illtyd Trethowan (New York: Holt, Rinehart and Winston, 1964), 154.

the light of their Creator. Just knowing that things are created helps us appreciate them in an altogether fresh way; the necessities of their nature and the contingency of their being show up in sharpest contrast against the background of the necessity of God and his freedom. Then too the light of revelation deals with the sin that obscures our view and mars the human realities we are trying to see. Third, we appreciate what nature is by contrast to what is above it. So, in healing and elevating nature, grace lets us see it, and live according to it, in a way not available outside the supernatural order.

But also, Christianity is not just a light, it is also a life. Grace lets us do what otherwise we cannot do, even when what we do is some naturally good and virtuous action. Promising for life, presupposing as it does a hold of both mind and will on some great life good, may be one of these things.

The Greeks, or some of them, Platonists and Stoics, knew of a transcendent good, or Logos, standing above as a sort of impersonal guarantor both of our moral judgments and of our moral undertakings. It was not a witness to our promising, since it had no eyes. It was enough shame to be seen by other men to fail by measure of this standard. Some people can keep a sense of the transcendence and objectivity of the Good apart from Christianity or Judaism and even after they have been renounced. Iris Murdoch could. But most people cannot.

To think along these lines means three things. First, we can be saddened but not surprised or dismayed by the divorce statistics in the United States or the large number of priestly defections in the United States since the Vatican Council or the emptying of cloister and convent. We have entered a world in which promising is harder. We should not expect marriage to be appreciated in the modern world as it was in the classical and Christian worlds. This means that married people trying to be married in the old way will have a harder go of it. And we should not be surprised that priests and religious lose their balance in a culture given over to sexual indulgence and the exaltation of a freedom that can never be bound.

Second, we Christians can stop trying to trim life promises to the modern world by hollowing them out and abandoning the very thing that makes them majestic and frightening and good in the first place, namely, the fact that they are for life. We do this by accepting divorce, either theoretically or in practice. We do this by not grieving the departure of priests and religious who fail to keep their promises. We do this by constantly calling into question the goodness of priestly celibacy. Hollowing out life promises from the inside means a practical and affective denial of the existence of the goods that make such promises possible in the first place.

Third, we must take up the hard work of catechesis, of showing the good, the goods, the Good that we engage in our promises. Religious, priestly, married vows are hard to keep. It is hard to keep the wedding garment put on at baptism for the feast of the Lamb unsoiled. It is the argument of this book that we keep our promises by keeping our eye on the good the promise intends and begins already to embrace from the moment the promise is made. "Let us turn now to encouragement, so that the good that is properly understood will be ardently loved," St. Augustine says to widows in order to help them keep their vows.[5] The good must first of all be seen. And of our Lord we read in the Letter to the Hebrews that he was one "Who for the joy that was set before him endured the cross, despising the shame" (12:2). Now, joy is an affective response to the good possessed. Our Lord fulfilled his mission, therefore, if not by vow, then by doing what we need to do to in order to vow and in order to do what we vow, namely, by keeping his eye on the good.

Above, it was claimed that Christ is both God's promise to us and our promise to God. Because of this, the point of being in Christ can be stated by saying that, for those who are in Christ, for those who love God, our promise to God is God's promise to us. For remember, we promise, not for God's good, but for our own. And our promise is at the will, call, gift of God. That is, when we promise in a religiously determined, Christianly determinate way, we take up a mission that contains our final identity, we take up a

---

5 *The Excellence of Widowhood,* in *Marriage and Virginity,* trans. Ray Kearney, *The Works of Saint Augustine: A Translation for the 21st Century,* I/9, ed. John Rotelle (Hyde Park, NY: New City Press, 1990), 126.

participation in Christ that is our destined good from the foundation of the world, we actualize the promise God makes us.

If we know our promises, the content of our promises, in this way, we will have the kind of knowledge of them that will move us to fulfill them with an ardor whose principle is the Holy Spirit. We will think the sufferings connected in this age with the discharge of our promises "not worth comparing with the glory that is to be revealed to us" (Rom 8:18). While we wait for the revelation of the sons of God and the redemption of our bodies (8:19, 23), the Spirit will help us in our weakness (8:26). Both the Spirit and Christ will intercede for us (8:27, 35), and we will not separate ourselves from the love of God in Christ Jesus our Lord. ∷

:::: Index

Proper Names and Subjects

Scripture